MW01119911

Charting a Profitable Investment Course with Active Management

A New Investment Paradigm for Expansions, Recessions & Everything in Between

BY ROBERT N. STEIN

Managing Partner and Senior Economist,
Astor Asset Management

MARKETPLACE BOOKS
Columbia, MD

ADVISOR
ESSENTIALS
SERIES

www.FPBooks.com

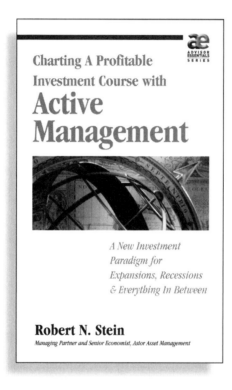

Charting A Profitable
Investment Course with
Active
Management

ae
ADVISOR
ESSENTIALS
SERIES

A New Investment
Paradigm for
Expansions, Recessions
& Everything In Between

Robert N. Stein
Managing Partner and Senior Economist, Astor Asset Management

"Rob expands on teaching us the importance
of disciplined investment strategies
to combat these turbulent market times,
so we don't make short-term mistakes
with our investments. He has a knack of
bringing light to complex concepts."

—Steve Gradeless
Nationwide Financial Services, Inc.

Titles in the Advisor Essentials Series

Published by Marketplace Books and distributed exclusively by www.fpbooks.com

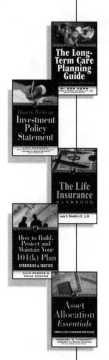

"Stock market investing is the hardest way to make an easy buck. Without knowledge and understanding of economics and the markets, I wouldn't put that buck at risk."

—Rob Stein

This book, along with many other books, is available at discounts that make it realistic to provide them as gifts to your customers, clients, and staff. For more information on these long lasting, cost effective premiums, please call John Boyer at (800) 272-2855 or you may email him at John@FPBooks.com

ISBN 1-59280-065-3

Printed in the United States of America.

1 2 3 4 5 6 7 8 9 0

Contents

Chapter 4

Chapter 5

Glossary of Economic Terms

Appendix

Recommended Reading

About the Author

Charting a Profitable Investment Course with Active Management

A New Investment Paradigm for Expansions, Recessions & Everything in Between

Acknowledgements

When sitting down to write a book it truly becomes a labor of love from so many sources, expected and unexpected. A simple thank you is never enough, but hopefully the meaningful words of gratitude mentioned here will somehow express the appreciation I have for their support.

My colleagues at Astor who work above and beyond the call of duty to give our clients the best service and products are truly dedicated to our cause. I am grateful to Bryan Novak who works countless hours on our proprietary models, always trying to improve upon what we have built. I owe Bryan a special thank you for his support and input on our case study, which really proves all that we preach in a very concise way. Another colleague of mine at Astor Asset Management is Scott Martin, who also contributed significantly to the case study. Scott has become invaluable for his input on the economic numbers. I have learned to rely on him for his instincts about economic data and his contribution to the weekly economic newsletter and interpretation of the daily economic data, which are updated in our economic calendar on the Astor website (www.astorllc.com).

I have recently been lucky enough to learn about the business of money management—or money management as a business, which is different than the money management business—from several seasoned professionals. My recent association with George Ball, former president of E.F. Hutton and current chairman of Sanders Morris Harris Group (SMHG), a Houston-based financial services firm, and his colleague Bill Floyd has taught me more about the business I so warmly embrace.

A writing project is not complete without support with the actual production of the manuscript. I thank Jaye Abbatte of Traders Library/Marketplace Books for seeing this project through and for many of the insightful ideas she had for the vision of this book. Further, a writing project of mine would never be complete without the help and guidance of my dear friend and colleague Tricia Crisafulli. Her ability to help with just the right words to fully express my thoughts continues to amaze me. I can't believe that Tricia doesn't have a degree in economics. Thank you, Tricia, for everything.

Of course support from outside business is also very important in completing this project. My family has always been supportive of me in almost all of my endeavors: my mother Baila, father Jerry, brother David, and sister Jeanne have become a personal support group, critic and cheerleader. My childhood friends from Lincolnwood and my grown-up friends from New York make succeeding all that more enjoyable. Last, but not least, is the support from my wife, Eileen, proving that achieving your goals is always better when there is someone to share them with.

I hope all enjoy this book and take away from it a new understanding of investing, the markets and the economy.

Thank you,
Rob Stein

Introduction — The New Investment Climate

lthough I think of myself as an economist first, I have always been interested and active in the markets. Over the years, I have been able to combine my study of the economy and the markets into a single discipline: investing based upon the economic cycle. This enables me, as an investor and a portfolio manager, to put the power of the "big picture" behind each investment decision.

From the start of my career as an intern at the Federal Reserve, then under the chairmanship of Paul Volcker, to my move to Wall Street where I was a senior trader for several prestigious banks, I saw the importance of economic data. Not only did the data influence the market, it determined the overall tone and direction of the market. I quickly saw that forecasting the economy, a capricious endeavor at best, was not as important for making on-target investment decisions as identifying the current stage of the economic cycle. Today, as a portfolio manager and managing director of Astor Asset Management, LLC, my emphasis remains on the current economic cycle.

Today's New Investment Climate

Focusing on the economy here and now is even more important given today's new investment climate. A distinctive feature of this new climate is that investment cycles will not be as pronounced, nor will they be as long in duration as prior cycles. As a consequence, these shortened cycles will have a significant impact on the economic order. For example, the most recent recession was shorter than the average over the past several decades. According to the National Bureau of Economic Research (NBER), the recession began in March 2001 and ended in November 2001. This 8-month duration was shorter than the average recession length of 11 months since World War II (excluding the 2001 recession).

This raises the key question of why the economic cycles are getting shorter. One reason is that enhanced technology and faster information inflows mean that the impact of a news event or economic report is disseminated and absorbed into the marketplace more quickly than ever before, thereby affecting actions and reactions far more rapidly than in the past. Previously, when an event hit the market—be it a surprise interest-rate hike announced by the Federal Reserve or a national disaster—the impact would be increased volatility for a sustained period of time. We might see the Dow rise or fall by 100 points, only to gyrate 50 or 75 points in the other direction, before equilibrium was reached that reflected the impact and outcome of that event or announcement. However, as we've seen in late 2003 and early 2004, the market has been adjusting much more quickly and efficiently to news events and their impact.

For example, consider when news broke in December 2003 of Saddam Hussein's capture. The market rallied quickly, then sold off just a few hours later when the euphoria faded and the reality remained that this event would do nothing to U.S. corporate earnings. It was fascinating to observe how quickly—in a matter of an hour or two—the market reached equilibrium.

Given the information explosion and heightened investor awareness of economic and news events, this pattern is not likely to change. In fact, shorter investment cycles will be with us for the foreseeable future. As a result, the next economic cycle will be far shorter than we've seen in the past, most notably the long bull run of the 1990s, followed by the sharp decline of 2000. In those time periods, the economy and the market were moving in distinct and obvious directions.

As we've seen in the early days of 2004, with the Dow well above 10,000, investors have returned to the equities markets with gusto.

However, given the new economic climate, the reality is they cannot anticipate that this will be the mid-1990s all over again. During those "good ol' days" of equity investing, the market's upward rise was so predictable it was almost boring. Not so in the new investment climate.

Active Management

With shorter, less pronounced, economic and stock-market cycles, investment professionals and their clients must be more vigilant than ever. They will need to be astute about the underlying condition of the economy and the likely impact on the stock market. Consequently, they must be agile in both their decision-making and their actions. In other words, in this new investment paradigm, investors need to embrace a new way of approaching and reacting to the market by applying a strategy called *active management*. Active management means taking a proactive approach to investing by utilizing fundamental and/or technical analysis to create value in a portfolio.

> **Active management means taking a proactive approach to investing by utilizing fundamental and/or technical analysis to create value in a portfolio.**

The benefit of active management is that it allows financial professionals and their clients to make profits in any type of market climate, regardless of market direction, volatility, or bull or bear conditions. Using an active management approach, investment professionals and their clients trigger investment decisions to either buy (going long) or sell (going short) the market, depending upon a set of predetermined criteria. This is markedly different than just relying on a buy-and-hold strategy or investing in a portfolio of supposedly diversified holdings. Furthermore, active management reduces risk by limiting losses during bear markets and providing a better base to build profits during bull markets.

For investment professionals and their sophisticated clients, active management is a necessary strategy to pursue an independent and empowered financial future. A real strength of active management is that it is highly adaptable to most investors' goals and investment styles.

There are many ways to pursue active management. Some portfolio managers may choose to use market benchmarks such as a moving average or 52-week highs and lows. Others may track other indicators such as investor sentiment or overbought/oversold indicators.

> **The critical and most important issue is for investors to dedicate a portion of their assets to active management—whatever the criteria for their decisions are.**

The critical and most important issue is for investors to dedicate a portion of their assets to active management—whatever the criteria for their decisions are. Through active management, investors and the advisors who counsel them are no longer held captive by traditional buy-and-hold strategies, and have an important defense against the vagaries of the stock market.

At my firm, Astor Asset Management, we take an economics-based approach to active management. In the simplest terms, this means

---

GOING LONG: Buying a stock, commodity, financial-futures contract or other instrument. With a long position, the investor is anticipating that the price of that instrument will rise when the market goes up. A profit is made when the instrument bought at a lower price is sold for a higher one.

GOING SHORT: Selling a stock, commodity, financial-futures contract or other instrument. With a short position, the investor is anticipating that the price of that instrument will decline when the market goes down. This is desirable because the short position makes a profit when what was sold at a higher price can be "bought back" at a lower price.

---

buying equities when the economic conditions are most favorable (economic expansion) and selling equities or even taking a short position in the market when the economic conditions dictate (economic contraction). Given the shorter economic cycles, there will also be gradations to our long and short positions. Thus, I must be prepared, depending upon our economic and market analysis, to be 75% to 100% long equities at times, and only 50% to 25% long at others, depending upon the strength of the cycle. Or, I may take a 25% short position in one market, such as the Nasdaq, while retaining a modest long position in another, such as the S&P 500. It's all determined by vigilantly analyzing economic indicators that signify the current stage of the economy (for example, whether we're in an expansion or a contraction), rather than reacting to the fluctuations of the market and the advice of TV pundits.

Through active management, investors and the advisors who counsel them are no longer held captive by traditional buy-and-hold strategies, and have an important defense against the vagaries of the stock market.

Being vigilant and flexible — ready to switch from a partially long to a partially short position and back again — will be the only way to reap a positive portfolio return in this decade. Investment professionals, and their clients who fail to recognize this, run the risk of having the gains from the bull cycles erased by the ensuing bear corrections, with shorter time frames to recoup their losses. If that happens, where will they be in the end?

Therefore, for the investment professional and the savvy investor alike, the new investment climate demands a new approach. One finger must be kept on the pulse of the economy and another on the trigger of investment decisions. Make no mistake: I'm not talking about capturing short-term moves that last only a few days. Rather, I'm proposing to be nimble enough in one's economic/market analysis and investment decisions to take on long and short positions as the conditions dictate.

Active management, I'm confident, is the new investment paradigm for today's economic climate, and the broad base of investors participating in the market. The stock market, once seen as an exclusive club for the wealthy, has seen wider participation than ever before, largely through the proliferation of 401(k) and other retirement accounts. Mutual funds, individual stocks and other securities make up the portfolios of more Americans than ever before. With their financial security on the line, these investors have become hyper-aware of the market conditions — especially given the painful lessons of 2000-2002 when investors learned the price of not paying attention to the market and the changing economic conditions. This is compounded by a myriad of investment choices available to investors and 24/7 access to global, national and economic news and events that can rock or rally the market. With investors so highly vested in the market, with their security of their futures literally on the line, adopting an active management strategy is imperative. As you'll read later in this book, active management can reduce risk and potentially improve returns in a far shorter time frame than the average returns associated with traditional strategies.

Benefits of Active Management

My purpose in writing this book is to explain the benefits of active management and how this approach is a vitally important tool for today's investment professionals and the clientele they serve. As you will read in Chapter 1, the days of the "do it all" broker/investment advisor have been eclipsed by an age of specialization. Those who excel at customer relationships will be the asset gatherers and allocators. Those who excel at portfolio management will manage those assets. In a complex market environment, this specialization also will allow each professional to focus on what he or she does best, while working in mutually beneficial relationships.

Chapter 2 will further explore the concept of active management and economics-based investing. Anyone who thinks of economics as a dull subject, full of dusty statistics, is in for a pleasant surprise. As readers of my Logical Economics newsletter know, economics is alive and vibrant, and a very necessary study for anyone who is serious about investing. By looking at economic factors such as gross domestic product (GDP) or unemployment, you can tell how well or poorly the economy is fairing. And since the state of the U.S. economy has the single greatest impact on the stock market, more than any other factor, it's crucial to monitor the economic forces at play, to keep your portfolio at peak performance. In this chapter, you'll not only learn how to put together the pieces of the economic puzzle, you'll find it interesting and even entertaining.

Chapter 3 will discuss how economics-based active management can be deployed in various portfolio scenarios, with an understanding of the client's risk-tolerance and investment objectives. This section will demonstrate the sheer versatility of active management.

As so many investors, and quite a few investment professionals, learned after the bull's stampede of the 1990s and the bear's rampage of 2000 to 2002, investing requires more than merely allocating assets and then walking away to let time do some sort of magic. Successful investing requires continual study and sharp decisiveness. As this book will illustrate, this doesn't mean you have to be tuned to the market's every move all day long. But it does mean that by monitoring a handful of key economic indicators you can be aware of shifts and undercurrents in time for you to react and preserve more of your hard-earned wealth. It is a discipline that cannot be underestimated, and, as we all know, its reward is well worth it.

Chapter 1

TIMES, THEY ARE A-CHANGIN' . . . AGAIN

The investment profession is in the midst of significant change, which is altering both the way we do business with clients, and the relationships among professionals. One of the outward signs of this change has been the abandonment of "buy-and-hold" as the predominant investment advice.

More accurately termed "buy and hope," this strategy worked fairly well into the 1990s. However, it is no longer meeting the demands of sophisticated investors or the savvy professionals who serve them. Today's confident and knowledgeable investors, with a wealth of online investing tools at their fingertips, became accustomed to the high yields and returns of the 1990s. They are still demanding high performance from their financial managers and advisors, even though times have changed. Given today's frequently fluctuating market conditions and shorter market cycles, it's an increasingly complicated task for financial professionals to deliver consistently high returns. Active management, therefore, provides an ideal alternative given the new investment paradigm.

Why? The reason is active management seeks to capitalize on all market trends regardless of direction. It provides greater returns over time with potentially less risk, and, most importantly, with a strategy to avoid significant drawdowns. We'll now explain how active management can work within an investor's portfolio.

Active management is a philosophy that empowers investors to take action to profit from market trends, regardless of direction. These actions may be based on many factors that can impact an investor's portfolio, such as the state of the economy, geopolitical events, money flows and market performance.

> **Active management is a philosophy that empowers investors to take action to profit from market trends, regardless of direction. These actions may be based on many factors that can impact an investor's portfolio, such as the state of the economy, geopolitical events, money flows and market performance.**

As stated in the introduction, there are many varieties of active management strategies. Some may follow market indicators such as moving averages. My firm, Astor Asset Management, bases its active management decisions on the state of the U.S. economy. Specifically, we determine whether the economy is expanding, which favors buying equities (long positions), or contracting, which necessitates selling (to take profits or to establish a short position). Whatever the strategy, investors would do well to dedicate a portion of their assets to active management, in order to reduce risk and reap potentially higher returns compared with buy-and-hold.

I'd like to emphasize that the definition of active management does not refer to a threshold number of transactions. Rather, it relates to participation in an active investment strategy that involves buying or selling decisions based on specific criteria. It is no longer enough for investors to make all the profits they can during bull markets and run for safety with the hope that losses aren't too bad during bear markets. Investors, who want not only to preserve profits, but also to build wealth, must be active in every market climate. Be it bull market or bear market, active management provides opportunities to make profits. Or at the very least, reduce losses.

Investors and investment professionals must also not confuse active management with trading (although some of the principles of active management can apply to trading). However, there is a place for trading, and many sophisticated market participants do trade within a portfolio. Active management, however, is an investment strategy that uses specific guidelines for making certain types of investment decisions, based upon a set of criteria and conditions.

That said, there is an important philosophic commonality between trading and active management. In trading, opportunities to profit are sought regardless of market direction. A trader of Nasdaq stocks or S&P futures is equally comfortable taking a long or short position and making money whether the market rises or falls. So, too, with active management. Each market—from equities to bonds to commodities—is evaluated on the basis of its specific events and conditions. A strategy is developed and implemented based on market analysis and indicators, allowing investors to establish positions during favorable times and to exit them when conditions change.

The New Era of Specialization

The new investment paradigm is placing greater demands on today's investment professionals. Demanding and discerning clients are seeking consistently strong returns to preserve their hard-earned wealth. Having weathered the storm of 2000 - 2002, they understand all too well that market corrections can be swift, painful and come at the worst times—specifically, wiping out half or more of their gains, at a time when their portfolios were at their peak.

To respond to these changing conditions, the world of the investment professional is being divided into three basic groups: the asset gatherer, who works closely with clients; the asset manager, who focuses on portfolio strategies, and the traditional broker. It's important to recognize how active management promotes cooperation and interrelationships among all these players, as the industry returns to an era of specialization.

In these times, those who excel at client relationships are spending their time and energy building and maintaining a client base. They are the asset gatherers. Those who are best at managing assets are

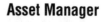

Asset Manager

Develops products and strategies.
Works with Asset Gatherers to offer
services — including active
management — to clients.

Asset Gatherer

Knows the client best.
Understands the client's needs.
Identifies investment strategies
and products offered by
Asset Managers.

Transaction-Based Broker

Essential to Active Manager to execute
strategy efficiently and inexpensively.
Understands the nuances of trading, including
block transactions, stop-loss orders,
short sales, delivery vs. payment
orders, margin/settlement
requirements, etc.

INVESTMENT PROFESSIONAL SPECIALISTS

focusing on investment strategies and products that can produce returns that are not correlated to stock-market movements. They are the asset managers. At the same time, traditional brokers, who in the 1990s made a lucrative living by picking and promoting the hottest stocks, are weaning themselves from their commissions in favor of fee-based services. Or, brokers are finding they play a key role with asset managers who are in need of their trade-execution services and expertise.

Brokers, investment advisors, and money managers can no longer be all things to all people. When it comes to providing client services, investment professionals are facing a choice of being either asset gatherers (building and managing client relationships) or asset managers (developing and offering investment services and products). By focusing on what they each do best, investment professionals will be better able to meet the increased demands of sophisticated investors.

Active management is not a new concept borne of the stock-market correction and economic contraction of 2000-2002. Traders and professional investors have traditionally followed a strategy of making profits regardless of market direction, producing returns that are not correlated to the stock market. The difference, however, is that this concept has now attained real meaning for the largest growing group of retail investors today.

After suffering the recent declines of the equity market, investors know it is not enough to guard against losses in a down market. And, equity diversification alone — once touted by the portfolio managers and financial planners as the key way to spread risk and protect rewards — is not sufficient. Investors have awakened to the fact that buy-and-hold does not carry the expected risk and returns that are acceptable to them. More investors want to be masters of their own financial fate, and they are asking investment professionals for the means to achieve these goals.

Moreover, investors don't want to wait for the next bull market to bail them out of bear-market losses with hopes of posting a net gain. In the parlance of the investment trade, they want to achieve returns that are not correlated with the stock market. To accomplish this, they are looking for active management strategies that will allow them to achieve their investment goals independent of the market's movements. Investors are becoming more open than ever before to alternative strategies, such as those entailed with active management. As

INDIVIDUALLY MANAGED ACCOUNTS: These accounts (also known as separately managed accounts) allow investors to have their assets individually managed, rather than commingled as in a mutual fund. There are several advantages to individually managed accounts, including a degree of customization within the portfolio manager's approach (such as how aggressively long, or short, an investor wishes to be, based upon risk parameters and other considerations). Individually managed accounts also can be managed for the optimum tax efficiency, compared with a mutual fund, which results in tax implications based upon the manager's buying and selling decisions.

evidence of this shift, consider the growth of individually managed accounts that are managed by third parties. To date, more than $400 billion has moved into individually managed accounts, an amount that is expected to exceed $2.1 trillion by 2011, according to a 2003 study by Financial Research Corporation.

I believe the growing popularity of individually managed accounts is a direct result of the losses that investors suffered in equities during the market downturn of 2000-2002. Led to believe that buy-and-hold was a suitable strategy for the long term, investors learned the hard way what happens when the market corrects at an inopportune time, specifically following a long market expansion that saw significant increases in portfolios. Investors who held equity-heavy portfolios — particularly the more risky technology and Internet stocks — were in for a rude awakening. All too often, the stocks that they had decided to "buy" were worth far less if they decided to "hold" onto them. The lesson in these losses, however, was that by taking a more proactive approach to the market by utilizing an active management approach, investors could seek ways to avoid costly downturns and build a greater degree of wealth for the future.

Striking a Partnership

For the investment professional, active management requires a partnership between the asset gatherer and the asset manager, drawing upon the strength of each party. These inter-relationships are facilitated through third-party investment advisor (TPIA) agreements. TPIAs typically charge a quarterly management fee, which is paid directly by the client, based on assets in the account. Depending on the advisory relationship, the asset manager will pay a portion of the management fee to the advisor, as a fee for referring and servicing the client. In order to pay or receive referral fees, the parties must hold the required NASD licenses.

The TPIA referral fee gives financial advisors an incentive to look for successful, suitable investment programs outside of their own practices, while allowing them to concentrate on customer service and attracting new clients. By establishing these relationships, the money or portfolio manager, can focus on performance and investment strategies, without the burden of client maintenance. This mutually

> **ASSET GATHERER:** Builds relationships with individual clients, based on a high degree of customer service and an ability to find investment strategies that meet the needs of the client. Referring clients to the right investment strategies requires a relationship between the asset gatherer and one or more asset managers, who are picked on the basis of their expertise, style of investment, risk parameters, and returns.
>
> **ASSET MANAGER:** Develops investment models and portfolio strategies, based upon a specific approach to the market. To offer these strategies and models, the asset manager needs relationships with several asset gatherers who refer clients. A third-party investment advisor (TPIA) agreement between the asset manager and the asset gatherer allows the two parties to share a quarterly management fee, paid by the client, based on assets.

beneficial relationship allows each party to efficiently and effectively grow its respective business.

But how did we get to such clear distinctions among financial professionals, that is, between the asset gatherer and the asset manager? It was only a few years ago, in the height of the stock-market craze, when everyone was trying to be all things to all clients. From financial planner, to asset gatherer, to commission-earning broker, everybody was in the stock-picking and advice-giving business. In the mid- to late-1990s, with the stock market soaring and so many people willing to believe the market would only go up, the time was ripe for distinctions among investment professionals to become blurred. Watching the market's steady rise, clients were demanding strong double-digit returns. Those expectations, coupled with the bull market, gave a strong incentive for everyone to be in the stock-picking game.

Of course, later, in the downturn, clients with high expectations exerted even more pressure on their advisors to produce returns, which many of them were hard-pressed to deliver. As investment professionals have come to realize, the best way to produce consistent returns, and protect against downturns, is for each party — the asset gatherer and the asset manager – to work together in a spirit of cooperation.

At this point, to fully appreciate these dynamic changes of late, we must look back a few decades. Understanding the full scope of evolution in the investment industry, we can appreciate where we are today, and where we are likely headed.

A Look Back in Investment History

The 1970s brought deregulation of brokerage commissions and the creation of the discount houses. These discount brokerages never gave advice per se, but rather offered retail clients low-cost and efficient execution on their investment transactions. This was the beginning of the separation between investment advice and investment execution. For clients who wanted to make their own investment decisions, the discount house was a welcome entrant into the field. Investors could buy and sell the stocks they wanted — when they wanted, and why they wanted — and pay a lower commission rate than that offered by a full-service broker. Of course, in time, even the discount houses would offer investment advice, but the legacy of the independent-minded investor who wanted a break on commissions was a lasting one.

The bull markets of the 1980s brought the first wave of new retail investors into the equity markets. Investors willingly opened brokerage accounts to buy stocks and hold them while they appreciated. The buy-and-hold passive investment strategy appealed to these new retail investors. What's more, in a steadily rising market, it made sense. Buy shares of some household-name companies, and hold for the long term. And if the stock prices fell a little, no matter! They'd make up for any losses over time. Or, as part of a dollar-cost averaging strategy, they saw the decline in price as another buying opportunity at a lower cost.

When it came to brokerage firms, stocks were the name of the game. Brokers didn't sell mutual funds in the early days; the fund companies marketed directly to retail investors. Mutual funds, however, appealed to a broader spectrum of investors, including those with smaller nest eggs to commit to the market. Through a mutual fund, these smaller amounts were pooled. Then, investors with only a few thousand dollars could own a stake in several companies to diversify their holdings. The market was experiencing an explosion in retail interest and participation.

Brokers who watched the flood of pooled assets pouring into mutual funds knew they were being shut out of the game. Mutual fund companies themselves realized they could extend their marketing reach through brokers. As a result, a separate class of fund shares was established, which paid a fee to the broker selling them. Now brokers had another arrow in their investment quiver: Not only could they recommend stocks, they could also offer a variety of mutual funds. Looking back, I see the introduction of C shares, or advisor shares as they are sometimes called, as the beginning of the "broker as your financial advisor" phase.

> **As mutual funds brought more investors into the marketplace, asset allocation became a household phrase, a concept that was embraced by financial planners, financial advisors, and many brokers to attract, educate, and maintain relationships with investors.**

As mutual funds brought more investors into the marketplace, asset allocation became a household phrase, a concept that was embraced by financial planners, financial advisors, and many brokers to attract, educate, and maintain relationships with investors. For the retail client, it made intuitive sense.

The concept of asset allocation was to put a little of everything on your investment plate, like walking through the line at a smorgasbord. Investors bought some blue chips and some growth stocks; they added a portion of small caps and some value stocks. With their money spread out over the various types of equities, investors felt they were increasing their odds of making a profit. Some stocks, after all, would do better than others, and the ones that performed exceptionally well would (hopefully) more than make up for those that only did so-so. There was no way of knowing which would be the star and which would be the laggard, since that could change over time. Hence, being "diversified" over many different types of stocks was seen as an easy and effective way of hedging one's bets.

Mirroring this desire to diversify among equity classes, mutual-fund companies launched products for virtually any sector imaginable, from Asia-only, to high technology, and everything in between. These sector funds gave brokers and investment advisors very popular products to sell to investors to accomplish asset allocation. Want more exposure in pharmaceuticals or biotechnology? What about ultra-aggressive small-cap growth? Or world funds with a smattering of stocks from around the globe? There were many funds to choose from, with ratings to show the best performers over a short or long time horizon.

Using sector funds, mutual funds and even bond funds, a broker could construct a diversified client portfolio, and that is precisely where the dichotomy among brokers began. On one side, there were brokers and advisors who used asset allocation to construct portfolios for their clients. They received a fee from mutual-fund companies for the funds that they sold. On the other side were the traditional brokers at the wire houses such as Merrill Lynch, recommending stocks and getting paid a commission for transactions.

These traditional brokers had stock picks from their in-house analysts to offer to retail clients. The stock analyst of the 1990s was taken out from behind the computer screen and put in the spotlight—literally. Their faces and names were seen regularly on CNBC. And any broker who was lucky enough to get the analyst's information first was suddenly in high demand.

These hot stock-picks further expanded the transaction side of the business, especially for the traditional wire house broker. The more active your clients, the more money you made. The more money you made on commissions, the more attention you attracted at the brokerage firm, which helped you to get better access to analyst information. That access to analyst information helped your clients find out about the hot stocks first-hand, instead of later on, when the information had already been disseminated, and the opportunity to buy ahead of the pack had disappeared. Fresher information and market advantage helped build and maintain the client base, which resulted in clients being more active and generating more commissions for the broker. The cycle went on and on . . .

In the 1990s, the transaction-based broker was generating significantly more revenue than the asset gatherer or the asset manager. This allowed the transaction-based broker to have fewer clients and less money under management. At the same time, the stock-market volatility and the constant need to find new ideas (and occasionally new clients) made the transaction-based broker only as good as his or her last month.

Meanwhile, the asset gatherers made their fees based on the service they provided and their access to good products. The fee they charged clients — normally a percentage of assets — didn't

> **By the end of the 1990s, at the height of the stock-market frenzy, it seemed every financial professional was at least partially in the transaction business, from traditional broker to asset gatherer.**

change all that much. But as long as the asset gatherer attracted new clients, he or she made more money. Also, as assets under management appreciated in value, the asset gatherer had a bigger base on which to draw a management fee. So, for example, if assets under management grew by 10%, the asset gather could count on a 10% increase in revenues from the management fee, even without attracting new clients. That allowed the asset gatherer to create a nice business that grew and generated revenue with the predictability of an annuity.

By the end of the 1990s, at the height of the stock-market frenzy, it seemed every financial professional was at least partially in the transaction business, from traditional broker to asset gatherer. Virtually everyone needed to be a stock picker, because clients were hungry

> In hindsight, we can see that investor appetites for the hot stocks and initial public offerings for the newest-idea-on-the-block.com led to some bad decisions on the part of investment professionals and their clients. In short, everyone had transaction fever.

for the next great stock to buy. The market itself made stock picking relatively easy. As the saying goes, a rising tide raises all boats, and the stock market was at high tide.

In hindsight, we can see that investor appetites for the hot stocks and initial public offerings for the newest-idea-on-the-block.com led to some bad decisions on the part of investment professionals and their clients. In short, everyone had transaction fever. Brokers willingly sent their client to web sites in order to do their own transactions or engage in trading. Even at a discounted rate, significant commission dollars were generated by clients who bought and sold stocks on a weekly—if not a daily—basis. The asset gatherer and the asset manager could not ignore the quest for transactions, and did their best to get in on the action with stock picks.

Investors opened multiple accounts, some for investing and others for short-term trading, buying today and selling a few days or weeks later when the stock price went up. At one time, there were said to be more accounts than there were investors! Some investors had their serious, long-term money relegated to one set of accounts. They also had some funds in "play accounts," just to dabble in "day trading" (which was actually short-term investing) on the side.

For some retail investors, and more than a few savvy individuals who should have known better, transaction fever clouded their judgment. Stories abounded of individuals who sold blue chips they had held for years in order to own the hottest technology stocks. People who had margin calls all too often didn't liquidate the supposed high-flying shares they were holding (even if they had deflated significantly);

instead, they sold their portfolio stalwarts to meet the margin calls. No matter if their grandparents had given them shares of GM twenty years before, if they needed to raise cash to meet a margin call or buy more of a Nasdaq stock that was already at a ridiculously high price/earnings ratio, they cashed in those blue chips without a second thought.

When it came to the hottest IPO, investors begged and pleaded with their brokers to get shares. That's when the amount of commission dollars generated really made a difference. Active investors, who wanted in on an IPO, weren't shy about reminding their brokers about how many commission dollars they had generated. Brokers also knew that IPOs were a very appealing carrot to offer their active investors: just keep trading with us and you'll get in on the next IPO. For investors, it always paid to be with the hottest brokers.

In the late 1990s, everybody and their mother loved to brag about the stocks they bought low and sold high. It was the financial version of the "fish story." The truth for many people, however, was that in the midst of a very volatile market, they bought a lot of overpriced stocks, bought even more when the price fell because they thought it was a bargain, and then bailed out of it all at breakeven.

I must confess that I bought an Internet stock called UUNET during its IPO. The stock, which was initially priced at $20 a share, ran all the way to $100 a share. I ended up selling at $70 a share. Sounds like I made a $50-a-share profit, right? Wrong. From $20 to $100 and back down again, I managed to buy and sell the shares at various prices. On a net basis, I barely broke even on a stock that, at its peak, was trading at five times its initial price.

Luckily I managed my investment portfolio far better than I did those UUNET shares. But I know I am not alone. The volatility of

The volatility of the market made for a lot of opportunities for savvy stock traders on the long and short side, and it made for a lot of losses for investors who ended up buying high and selling low.

the market made for a lot of opportunities for savvy stock traders on the long and short side, and it made for a lot of losses for investors who ended up buying high and selling low.

Investors were generally not concerned in the summer of 2000. We were in the midst of the Internet-dominated, technology-based new economy. Sure growth would be faster or slower at times, many investors thought. But was there really any fundamental reason for the economy to contract ever again? What a bill of goods investors tried to sell themselves!

When the Bubble Burst

What looked like a mere hiccup to some—a momentary correction in an overheated market—was the beginning of things to come. By the end of the third quarter of 2000, the market was in a downturn. There was no denying that the cycle had changed from an expanding economy that bolstered the stock market to a contracting economy that would take its toll on equities.

> **For the investment community, the ultimate trying time is a bear market.**

At Astor, we watch economic cycles very closely to determine our investment strategy (as I'll discuss in greater detail in Chapter 2). By the end of the third-quarter of 2000, we saw the classic economic signs of a contraction: stock prices were down, unemployment was rising, and the rate of growth as measured by GDP was lower.

As Thomas Paine, whose writings helped stir up the American Revolution, wrote, "These are the times that try men's souls." For the investment community, the ultimate trying time is a bear market. When the market turned downward in 2000 and into 2001, asset gatherers found that clients needed an inordinate amount of hand-holding as they watched the size of their holdings shrink. For the asset manager, especially those who were following a buy-and-hold/equity diversification strategy, the falling market was reflected in declining returns. This underscored the inherent problem with "buy and hope." While that strategy generally works well during the bull market and economic expansion, it became a problem when the economy began to contract and the market went south.

When the market sold off initially in 2000-2001, transaction-based brokers still made their commissions as nervous clients sold their holdings. Then customers shied away from buying, and transactions began to suffer. When clients started getting more margin calls, the transaction-based broker was finding the job of customer service to be a particularly difficult and challenging one.

The portfolio manager also saw a downturn in the value of assets under management, and may have felt the pinch as nervous clients bailed. And so it continued through the ranks of the investment industry. As the market moved lower still into 2001 and 2002, no one was spared at least a portion of the agony: brokers, investment advisors, mutual-fund managers, financial planners, and all the rest.

One result of all this was that the market's downward move debunked the myth of buy-and-hold once and for all. In an up market some sectors outperform the others. A downturn, however, is a different story. Aggressive growth stocks may have been hit first and the hardest, but in time no equities were spared. Not the blue chips. Not the value stocks. The diversified equity portfolio offered no shelter.

Real Diversification and Active Management

If there was one, single important lesson to be learned from the latest bear market, it was the value of *real* diversification, not just spreading equity exposure around to different types of stocks and adding some fixed-income holdings. The only strategy that proved viable during this period—and the one that holds the most promise for the ensuing uptrend as well—was true asset diversification through active management.

Active management matured as more asset classes became appropriate to invest in, including currencies, commodities, and hedge funds. Sophisticated investors with assets to devote to active management strategies were the target of the investment professionals, leaving the average investor with investment strategies that really weren't the best. Moreover, a brain drain was experienced as fund managers and money managers applied their talent and efforts to developing hedge funds and alternative strategies for an elite clientele—and the possibility to earn higher management fees and a share of the profits.

Seeing this opportunity to serve the retail traditional investor—just when this group needed it the most—new money-management firms were launched, including my own, Astor Asset Management, LLC, providing asset management through individually managed accounts. The goal of these new money-management firms was to bring alternative investment strategies to the traditional investor.

> **Investing in the broader indices is a far more effective way to profit from opportunities in bull and bear markets than trying to pick individual stocks.**

Over time, active management went from being a limited, niche product—such as hedge funds that catered to very wealthy investors—to opportunities for a wider retail audience. Even mutual funds entered the active management business, with firms such as Rydex Investments offering funds that replicate a long or a short position in S&P 500 or Nasdaq 100, simply by buying a mutual fund.

At Astor, active management means using economic analysis to determine the most opportune times to buy and sell equities: namely, we buy during economic expansions and sell—or even short-sell—during economic contractions. We accomplish this by utilizing investment instruments that represent a broader sector of the market, such as the S&P 500 or the Nasdaq 100. As explained in detail later in the book this can be done by using mutual funds and exchange-traded funds (ETFs) that track the major market indices.

We believe that investing in the broader indices is a far more effective way to profit from opportunities in bull and bear markets than trying to pick individual stocks. Granted, traditional wisdom says that even in a bear market there will be some "good" stocks to buy, and in a bull market the majority of stocks go up, although some to a greater degree than others. I believe the onus of picking the right stock for market conditions is far too risky with not enough reward. By contrast, applying active management to broader market indices increases an investor's chances of participating in the overall market trends, both up and down.

Certainly equities aren't the only instruments for an active management strategy. There are also alternatives for the fixed-income market. For example, the Income Appreciation Program at Astor offers clients a low-risk means to invest in the fixed-income markets.

Given the dominance of equities in most investor portfolios these days, it's extremely important to recognize how active management can potentially produce significant returns that are at least commensurate with the long-term, historical return of 12% to 15% over time, associated with stocks. Active management carries less risk than buying and holding stock, since it eliminates exposure to equities during market corrections. More aggressive investors can get short equities to capitalize on market corrections.

If you lose 50% of your portfolio, you need a gain of 100% just to get you back to flat. Based on average returns, this can take you eight to 10 years.

Active management is certainly in line with the basic investment concept of "buy low, sell high." After all, that is the fundamental way of making a profit. The vital difference, however, is that active management does not use arbitrary price targets or the fact that the market is up or down at a particular moment to trigger investment actions. Rather, it relies on preset criteria—in the case of Astor, the stages of the economic cycle—to make informed, intelligent investment decisions.

The buy low, sell high mantra, however, also plays into the myth of buy-and-hope. When investors buy, they obviously believe (and hope) that the value of whatever they purchased will go up over time, enabling them to sell at a higher price and book a profit. The problem comes in when the market drops unexpectedly. The investor is left holding onto something that is worth less than when he bought it. The solution that far too many investors take is to "hold on," believing that things will turn around eventually.

The bigger problem is that as the recent bear market has shown us, corrections in the overall stock market can come at the worst time, taking away 50% or more of an equity portfolio and wiping away years of gains. Unfortunately, these corrections occur when investors have their largest exposure to stocks, making the corrections feel even greater than their percentages. If you lose 50% of your portfolio, you need a gain of 100% just to get you back to flat. Based on average returns, this can take you eight to 10 years. Therefore, avoiding the drawdowns caused by contractions can add years to your investment life. Buy-and-hold, which once looked so safe, is obviously a far riskier strategy than investors and investment professionals thought a decade ago.

Active management unshackles investors from the market's movements. Rather than waiting for the market to turn around, investors can seek ways to make money in bull or bear conditions. For the investment professional, helping clients to understand the importance of active management can lead to more satisfying and profitable customer relationships.

Summary

At this point, let's sum up the changes that we've seen thus far in the investment business.

Investment professionals today must understand the implications of active management. Whether broker, advisor or money manager, the roles have become more defined. In today's markets, it is virtually impossible to be all things to all people. It used to be enough for a broker to have live quotes in the office in order to tell clients where certain stocks were trading or what "looked good" today. That is no longer the case.

Portfolio managers who used their performance figures and stock-picking abilities to impress clients are finding that the bar has been raised. Managing client relationships—answering phone calls from individuals weekly and sometimes daily—eats away at the manager's ability to focus on his or her strength: deploying an active management strategy.

Investment professionals must identify their strengths and operate from that basis. Are they best at building and maintaining client relationships, offering clients a variety of investment choices? If so, then their role is asset gatherer. Are they best at developing investment products, actively managing investments, and managing a portfolio? If so, then their role is asset manager.

A shift in the investor mindset is also promoting this type of specialization. Over the past 24 to 36 months, most brokers and investment advisors have seen a noticeable shift in the nature of their relationships with their clients. Rather than being asked for a stock pick, brokers and advisors are getting more calls from sophisticated clientele looking for strategic investment advice. They may have heard of a portfolio manager and want the investment advisor's opinion on the program.

> **The unifying goal today for all investment professionals is a commitment to providing a valuable service to clients.**

Today's sophisticated investor wants to reap the benefit of this specialization. This presents an opportunity to educate investors about exploring alternative strategies and investments that are not correlated with the stock market. Clients do not expect their broker or investment advisor to do that kind of active management on their behalf. Yet their brokers and advisors are very important to clients, helping them to pursue the right investment strategies that meet their financial goals and match their risk criteria. Brokers and advisors will be the gateway to helping investors find the right portfolio managers to get that job done.

The unifying goal today for all investment professionals is a commitment to providing a valuable service to clients. This is not a one-size-fits-all proposition. Some clients want to know how to invest on a short-term time frame and are interested in specific stocks. A broker who has specific experts on whom to rely, excellent information, and the latest technology to execute trades would best serve that individual. Clients who cannot stomach the gyrations of the market, and prefer to have a higher certainty of performance in any given quarter, or any given year, want to work with an advisor who can offer better products and advice to meet their particular goals. Likewise, the asset manager, with a greater number of sectors to exploit, and products and strategies to employ, has better tools to offer to clients, working in partnership with brokers and investment advisors.

> **Active management certainly isn't the solution for every client in every situation. It is, however, the cornerstone of the relationship between the asset gatherer, who knows the client best, and the asset manager who can meet the client's need for true, active diversification.**

From the biggest names on Wall Street to the smallest of boutiques, products and services have become increasingly client-driven. Funds, investment strategies and products are being rolled out in direct response to what clients want. This is a sharp departure from the 1990s when products were created first and sold to clients second.

Active management certainly isn't the solution for every client in every situation. It is, however, the cornerstone of the relationship between the asset gatherer, who knows the client best, and the asset manager who can meet the client's need for true, active diversification. Through active management, investment professionals will be able to offer their clients more opportunities to win, instead of just hoping that the underperformance in one area of their portfolio will be made up by the return in another.

Here's an analogy that illustrates this point: A football team with a strong offense can score enough touchdowns to win the game. But a football team with a pretty good offense and a pretty good defense can potentially score regardless of who's on the field. The offensive team will get its share of touchdowns, and the defensive team will create turnovers and run with the ball—while keeping the other team from scoring. In the end, the team that has both a good offense and a good defense will likely have the better score and win the game.

Certainly active managers, including Astor, will not be able to score every time. They will have their share of market fumbles and under-performance. Nonetheless, the only way for investment advisors and brokers to add value—and for investors to take advantage of all market opportunities—is with a series of actively managed accounts in a variety of asset classes. This is the power of true diversification. Diversifying among asset classes, and then actively managing each of those asset classes, offers the highest potential to increase return, reduce risk and shorten the time frame to achieve investment goals.

Chapter 2

ACTIVE MANAGEMENT AND ECONOMIC REALITY

To actively manage an account or portfolio, you need criteria for when to buy and when to sell. Unlike buy-and-hold, the key ingredients of which are time and hope, active management is predicated on decisions for when to be long, when to be short, and when to be in cash and waiting for the next opportunity. At my firm, Astor Asset Management, our active management strategy is based on one important factor. The economy.

Specifically, we invest based on the current economic conditions, not what we believe the economy is likely to do a few months from now. As I have found over the years, the economic *reality* is far more powerful than a *hypothetical forecast*. I learned this first-hand when I started my career as an analyst at the Federal Reserve. Part of my job was to compile economic data, dealing with tangibles such as the rate of growth of the GDP, weekly jobless claims, or the size of the U.S. workforce.

When I moved to Wall Street, I took on a much more difficult job: forecasting. The problem with forecasting was that I was wrong a lot. It's like the old joke that says economists were created to make the weather-forecasters look good. Very quickly I returned to my analytical roots. Rather than trying to forecast what was going to happen, I wanted to review and analyze economic data to determine what was happening at the time. Specifically, I wanted to create criteria to determine the current stage of the business cycle—expansion, peak, contraction, or trough. Once the business cycle was identified, an active management investment strategy could be implemented to capitalize on that particular stage.

I decided to base my career on being able to read economic data and determine what it was saying about current conditions. As a result, I became far less concerned about what would likely happen next quarter or next year. Now, as a portfolio manager, I use active management based on current economic conditions, which I believe is a far more satisfying approach to investment.

The Business Cycle

Determining the current phase of the business cycle is not without its challenges. For one thing, economic signals can be mixed, and the economy can grow (or contract) at different rates at different times. The objective, therefore, is to look at specific economic data, which I'll review later in this chapter, and make a determination of where the economy is at the moment.

At any given time, the economy is in one of four sequential phases of the business cycle—expansion, peak, contraction, and trough. Repeated over and over through the decades, the business cycle looks like a sine wave rising higher, peaking out, declining, hitting

ECONOMIC SINE WAVE

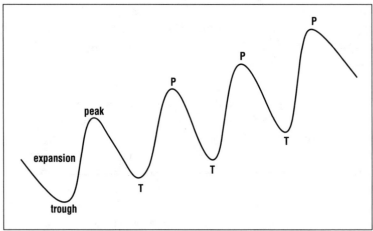

bottom, and rising again. The overall direction of the wave is upward, with higher peaks and higher bottoms as well, as the U.S. economy moves steadily forward.

Let's take a look at each of these four phases and the discerning characteristics of each:

- **Expansion** usually lasts the longest of all the economic stages, and produces the greatest amount of wealth. This phase is marked by low unemployment and higher corporate profits, which usually lead to stock-market rallies. In simplest terms, when more people are working, producing more things, and investing more money, these are the signs of an expanding economy.

- **Peak** is the euphoria stage during which stock prices appreciate sharply and consumer spending surges. This is also when companies tend to overbuild, overbuy and over-hire. Excesses build up that are not healthy for the economy in the long run.

- **Contraction** may be an unpleasant stage, but it is a very necessary one. As the economy slows down or slips into recession, businesses begin to shed the excesses that resulted from expansion/peak stages. Consumer spending and investment decreases. Companies lay off workers and stock prices decline. Contraction is the mirror opposite of expansion. In simplest terms, it means fewer people working, less stuff being made, and a decline in investment.

> At any given time, the economy is in one of four sequential phases of the business cycle—expansion, peak, contraction and trough.

- **Trough** is when the contraction "hits bottom." Large numbers of workers are laid off, and consumer spending declines. Although the economy is still contracting during the trough, companies that are leaner and more efficient start to make money again. Lower labor costs and higher worker productivity (the result of earlier layoffs) help boost corporate profits. This allows the economy to get healthy again and starts the cycle back to expansion.

Defining the Business Cycle in Real Time

The business cycle is easiest to identify in the rearview mirror. With the passage of time, economists study not only the current economic data, but also the latest numbers in the context of previous data. That's why the National Bureau of Economic Research (NBER) makes its pronouncements on the beginning and end of a recession months after the fact.

From an active-management standpoint, the challenge is to determine how the economy is performing *right now*. Do the data indicate an expanding economy or a contracting one? Is the data mixed, indicating the next phase is not fully underway? While there is a plethora of data by which to analyze the economy—from Durable Goods and Vehicle Sales to reports from regional Federal Reserve banks—we at Astor have broken it down to the "ABCs" of economic analysis to make our determination. They are:

- GDP
- Employment
- Investment money flows/stock-price momentum

Using this data we are trying to determine if more people are working (as measured by employment statistics) and making more stuff (as measured by GDP), and investing more money (as measured by money flows/stock-price momentum). If so, then the economy would be expanding. Conversely, if fewer people were working, making less stuff and investing less, then the economy would be contracting.

Let's take a closer look at each of these components of our economic analysis.

GDP

GDP (Gross Domestic Product) is one of the most comprehensive measures of economic health in the United States, reflecting the physical output of U.S. businesses. Even though GDP is a lagging indicator that is subject to revision, it is a vitally important gauge of the economy that is watched by everyone from the Federal Reserve Board of Governors to traders on the stock-exchange floor. Granted, GDP does have some limitations: For example, it tends to understate the service and technology sectors, and it subtracts from U.S. output the goods and components imported into the U.S. by American multinationals from their overseas operations. Nonetheless, since those limitations are consistent quarter-to-quarter, GDP acts like an index, reflecting the relative strength or weakness of the economy.

To get technical just for a moment, GDP reflects the sum of consumption, investment, government spending and exports, minus imports. Of these components, the largest is consumption, accounting for about two-thirds of the total. Little wonder, then, that consumer spending is so closely watched.

You don't have to be an economist to decipher GDP or to understand what's happening "behind the scenes" in the economy. When a GDP report is released, the first questions to be considered are: How is the economy performing compared with the previous quarter? How does the economy compare with a year ago? Is the GDP rate of growth increasing, which would indicate relative improvement in the economy? Or, is the rate of growth declining, which shows that economic growth has slowed down?

Occasionally, GDP "goes negative," showing a quarterly growth rate such as -1.0%. Obviously, that doesn't mean the industrial production

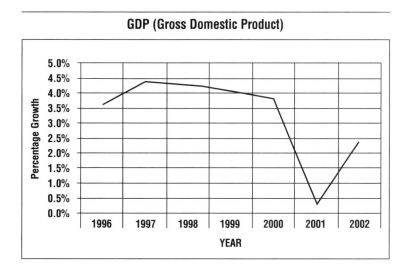

GDP (Gross Domestic Product)

> **A negative GDP reading is a sure sign of a contracting economy.**

plants have kicked into reverse and factories are now "unmaking" goods. Rather, it means that the rate of production has declined, in the most recent period, from the previous quarter. A negative GDP reading is a sure sign of a contracting economy. By classic definition, a recession occurs when there are two, sequential, negative GDP quarterly numbers. Increasing unemployment and declining stock prices, which can be just as painful as a classic recession, also characterize economic contractions.

Another insight that can be gleaned from the GDP report is the level of inventories. Inventories are not part of the GDP equation since goods in the warehouse today were previously counted as output. Nonetheless, the report does make note of inventory levels, which can influence the interpretation of a GDP number. For example, a strong GDP output number looks "less rosy" if growth in output resulted in higher inventories instead of increased consumer/end user sales. Further, when inventories decline because consumption has increased, it's a sign that economic activity may be picking up soon.

Employment

Employment has a broad impact beyond the immediate economic implications. Who has a job, who doesn't, and who is still looking are all very important and emotional considerations for the economy. People who have lost their jobs, or who are afraid of losing them, are reluctant consumers, and they certainly are far less likely to commit to any big-ticket purchases. (Remember, consumption is a big economic driver, accounting for two-thirds of GDP.) Jobless fears can also sour investor sentiment.

Employment is such an integral part of the economy that it is specifically mentioned by The Federal Reserve in its goals of monetary policy, as stated on the Federal Reserve web site (www.federalreserve.gov). "The Federal Reserve Act...specifies that, in conducting monetary policy, the Federal Reserve System and the Federal Open

Market Committee should seek 'to promote effectively the goals of maximum employment, stable prices, and moderate long-term interest rates'."

In addition, employment is tied directly to the business cycle. In a contracting economy, growth in demand slows and inventories build. Companies cut back production and lay off workers. This helps companies to reduce their labor costs, become more efficient and improve profitability. During a recession, worker productivity (output per employee) typically improves. As the economy recovers and demand picks up, companies can benefit from lower labor costs for a time. Eventually, however, demand will reach the point at which production must be expanded and additional workers hired. Initially, productivity will decline. However, expansion in payrolls signals that economic recovery is underway.

> **What's most significant about productivity after an economic contraction is the degree to which the benefits linger.**

What's most significant about productivity after an economic contraction is the degree to which the benefits linger. For example, let's say a company has 100 workers making 100 widgets a day. When the economy contracts and demand slackens off, the company is forced to lay off workers. At first, there are 70 workers making 70 widgets a day, and then 50 workers making 60 widgets a day. This initial productivity increase is to be expected, but it's nothing to get excited about, because output is still down. When demand picks up, the company may be able to produce 70 widgets with those 50 workers before it must start hiring again. If the company has truly improved productivity, it will be able to increase production at a faster rate than it must hire workers. For example, if production eventually grows to 150 widgets produced by 100 workers—perhaps through more efficient manufacturing methods or a better use of technology—that's a significant productivity improvement. While contractions are painful, they can often result in better and healthier economic growth in the long run.

UNEMPLOYMENT RATE

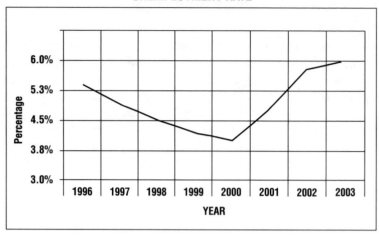

To decipher what's happening to the economy in terms of employment, attention is focused on the monthly Employment Situation Report, as it's officially known. When this report is released, the statistic that gets the most attention is the unemployment rate. The absolute statistic is not as important as the relative change from one month to the next and over a longer period of time. Another key statistic is the size of payroll employment, which reflects the rise or fall in the number of people working. Additionally, the report shows the number of newly unemployed persons, those who have been out of a job for less than five weeks.

The Employment Report is carefully tracked not only for what it reveals about the current labor market, but also for indications of how well or poorly the economy is performing. Increased joblessness, an increase in the number of newly unemployed persons and a shrinking of the payroll number are all indications of poor or weakening economic conditions. Similarly, an uptick in job creation, a decrease in the number of newly unemployed people, and growth in the payroll number are signs of economic improvement. Keep in mind that the economy needs to add about 1 million jobs a year to keep growing, taking into account both new entries and people leaving the workforce.

Investment Money Flows/Stock-Price Momentum

Investment Money Flows/Stock-Price Momentum reveals the underlying belief of how well the economy is performing. Typically, investor sentiment improves in step with economic growth and a better employment picture. The stock market, in fact, is one of the most important indicators of economic activity, reflecting both the outlook for growth in corporate output and profitability, and the mood of investors.

When analyzing the stock market, we are not concerned at all about price-to-earnings (P/E) ratios, which some analysts use to suggest whether a stock is under-priced, fairly valued or over-priced. In fact, we don't put much credence in P/E at all. Whether a stock is priced at $50 or $100, means little. Far more important is the relative change in stock prices — particularly when looking at the broader market. That's why we focus on the *direction* of money flows/stock price momentum.

> **The stock market is one of the most important indicators of economic activity, reflecting both the outlook for growth in corporate output and profitability, and the mood of investors.**

To our way of thinking, it's far more important to know if additional investor money is going into equities and increasing the value of the stock market, as reflected in the major indices such as the Dow, Standard & Poor's 500, or the Nasdaq Composite. Or are investors pulling out of equities, causing stock prices to decline? In some instances, the stock market's behavior may be more telling than the economic data, particularly when the economy is perceived to be at or near a turning point in the trend — in other words the peak or the trough.

A case in point: As the economy appeared to be continuing to deteriorate in the first quarter of 2003, the Nasdaq actually ended that quarter with a gain. In fact, the Nasdaq was up for two consecutive quarters, despite uncertain economic news, and, in particular, a persistently poor employment picture. From the perspective of the Nasdaq performance, however, the worsening employment picture was actually good news for certain companies, namely the high-tech firms dominating this sector. By Q1 2003, enough jobs had been cut and sufficient excess was pared back to the benefit of Nasdaq-traded companies.

When bad news is good for stocks seems to be a paradox. After all, during the initial phases of a contraction, bad economic news—such as a decline in GDP or higher unemployment—certainly tends to weigh heavily on the market. But during the latter phases of a contraction, it is often perceived as good news, at least for portions of the market. The companies that had to improve are taking their bitter medicine. As we'll discuss later in this chapter, the rally that was initially seen in Nasdaq didn't spread to the broader sectors until the middle of Q2 2003, when the momentum in other stock indices also turned decidedly positive. By later in the year, the economic data—with a stronger GDP and an improving employment picture—was in sync with improved stock-market performance.

When studying economic data or stock-market performance, it's important to look beyond just a single report or a one-month time frame. Trends are developed over time, and it often takes several months for a new trend to be identified and confirmed. With a longer-term perspective, the goal is to look for a consensus among the indicators, not only to confirm the trend, but also to gauge its strength. For example, when economic indicators show strong growth and the stock market is showing positive upward momentum, the conditions favor a sustained economic expansion. Conversely, when economic indicators worsen and the stock market turns downward, the stage is set for a sustained contraction.

Participating in the Broad Market

Once the current business cycle is identified, an investment strategy can be put in place. While these strategies have many variations, depending upon factors from the age of the investor to his or her risk tolerance (which will be discussed in Chapter 3), there are two basic investment premises that should be followed:

- An expanding economy is favorable to equity markets and therefore owning stocks.

- A contracting economy is unfavorable for equities, and therefore stocks should be sold and/or short positions taken, and/or increasing allocations to bonds and cash.

What is the best way to establish a long or short position in the equity market to capitalize on the current economic condition using an active management strategy? In my mind, there is no better way to participate in the stock market's moves—both bullish and bearish—than with the broader indices. These indices, such as the Standard & Poor's 500[1] (S&P 500) and Nasdaq 100[2], are better surrogates for the U.S. economy as a whole than any one particular stock.

That's not to say stocks have no place in an investor's portfolio. Many investors buy stocks that they like or that they purchase because of

---

1 S&P 500 is a registered trademark of McGraw-Hill, Inc.
2 Nasdaq 100 is a registered trademark of The Nasdaq Stock Market, Inc.

Standard & Poor's 500: The S&P 500 is a basket of 500 widely held stocks, weighted by market value and performance. The index is designed to be representative of the stock market as a whole. Company stocks are selected for the index based upon their market size, liquidity and sector (such as financial, technology, etc.). The S&P 500 is widely used to judge overall U.S. market performance and as a benchmark for performance used by portfolio managers and investment professionals.

Nasdaq 100: The Nasdaq 100 is a weighted index of the top 100 non-financial stocks traded on The Nasdaq Stock Market. The Nasdaq 100 is a narrower index than the Nasdaq Composite, an index that reflects the value of all the stocks traded on the Nasdaq. Dominated by the leading, large-cap technology stocks, the Nasdaq 100 is often used as a benchmark for technology-stock performance.

potential growth in a particular sector of the economy. When it comes to active management, however, I believe that the best way to capture the movements of the overall economy is with broad-based indices like the S&P 500 or Nasdaq 100. Keep in mind that active management involves a portion of an investor's portfolio. As I'll explain in Chapter 3, active management may account for 40% to 60% of an investor's *equity* holdings. Depending upon the portfolio mix, this may be as little as 20% or as much as 40% of the overall portfolio.

It's also important to realize that the primary determining factor of a stock's movement is the underlying direction and momentum of the broader equity market. In fact, industry data show the market itself may account for nearly 80% of a stock's movement. Wouldn't it be more efficient and effective to participate in the broad market through a stock index? An index, by definition, will reflect a large sector of the economy. This cannot be accomplished with any confidence by picking individual stocks. Even in a roaring bull market, there is always the chance that the one stock an investor picks is a laggard.

Investors can use a variety of products that reflect the performance of the specific indexes. These include exchange-traded funds (ETFs), such as iShares, which replicate a variety of indices. In addition, there are index mutual funds that replicate both long and short positions in the indexes. There are advantages and disadvantages with each.

Exchange-Traded Funds (ETFs): These are traded instruments that track a particular index. An ETF acts just like a regular stock, enabling investors to take a long position by buying shares in the ETF, or a short position by selling (or short selling) the ETF. Further, because ETFs are traded on stock exchanges, they can be bought and sold at virtually any time, at prices that fluctuate just like those of any stock. Examples of ETFs include the Standard & Poor's Deposit Receipt (SPDR), known as "Spiders," which tracks the S&P 500. Similarly, the QQQs is an ETF that tracks the Nasdaq 100. Barclays Global Investors' iShares are a large family of ETFs that provide exposure to a number of indices.

Mutual funds have higher fees than the costs associated with ETFs. Through mutual funds, however, one can obtain the net asset value (NAV) at the end of each day for accounting and reporting purposes. In addition, investing with a mutual fund company through an advisor or manager does provide an additional safety net. Further, mutual funds that replicate an inverse position in a particular index allow an investor to hold the equivalent of a short position, without having to deal with margin or establishing a short position.

The Active Management Advantage

For today's savvy investment professional and discerning clientele, active management is a valuable tool. Active management holds the key to attaining higher performance at lower risk than the traditional buy-and-hold approach. Allow me to explain: Statistically, with buy-and-hold an investor could make an average return of 9 to 11 percent per year over the long term. During the course of holding stocks, however, there is a high likelihood of suffering a 50 percent correction/drawdown. Unfortunately, you do not know when that loss will occur. Very often it follows the peak of your account holdings, and results in losses that will take years to make up. If your account loses 50 percent, you would need to reap a 100-percent return, just to get back to even. At a 10-percent average-annual return, that would take nearly a decade. To my way of thinking, the 9 to 11 percent return over the long run is just not worth the gyrations that would have to be endured in the meantime.

> **During the course of holding stocks, there is a high likelihood of suffering a 50 percent correction/drawdown.**

For the investment professional, it's clear that active management strategies are valuable tools for delivering performance to clients, with fewer headaches during the downturns. Further, when the downside risk during corrections is limited (or potentially eliminated altogether), clients have a stronger base on which to build wealth over a shorter time horizon, compared with buy-and-hold.

The key to active management is that it offers strategies whereby investors can potentially avoid most of the drawdowns by getting out of equities during adverse economic times—or even taking a short position to capitalize on a declining market. While investors won't catch every up-move in the market, as they switch from a short to a long position when economic analysis dictates, they won't need to. Over time, losses will be smaller, and investors will be allowed to reap profits with short positions during market corrections, and to hold profitable long positions during market appreciation.

As part of economics-based active management, it's important to let the analysis do the work that it's supposed to do. In other words, you can't become so wedded to ideas or perceptions of what you think is happening—or what you think *should* be happening—that you fail to do the analysis or take it seriously. That doesn't mean you make an investment choice based on every piece of new economic data. Rather, you must always survey the economic landscape to determine what is happening. When that picture is mixed, or the data is unclear, don't be afraid to sit on the sidelines until you can determine the economic trend with more confidence. There is nothing wrong with being out of the market, and in cash, until you feel more certain of what the economic data and stock-market performance are telling you.

> **When in doubt, get the heck out. That's a good mantra for the active investor and for professionals who advise them.**

When in doubt, get the heck out. That's a good mantra for the active investor and for professionals who advise them. No money was ever "lost" by being in cash. If it turned out you sold "too early," then all you did was forsake some potential profit. If you wait on the sidelines "too long" before getting in, you can still make significant profits as the trend continues. Consider what happened after the 1990-1991 recession. If you had waited until late 1994 or early 1995 before taking a position in equities—missing three years of the expansion—you still would have tripled your money in the S&P and made

10 times your money in the Nasdaq. That is, if you did one thing—sell when the expansion ended.

When people ask me what's the hardest part of investing, my answer is usually the same. It's not about picking good investments; it's about getting out of bad investments. The tendency of most investors is to hang on and wait for things to turn around. But while they wait, the stock they bought for $30 or $40 (or more) is dropping to $20 or $15.

Making Investments Based on Economics

By taking an active management approach with economic-based investing, investment professionals and their clientele have a firm rationale, and a more precise strategy for the decisions they make. This investment strategy is based upon underlying economic trends, not merely the fact that a particular stock or sector looks good at the moment. If the economy is expanding, it's a good time to be invested in equities, including higher-risk issues that tend to perform best during these times. When the economy is contracting, it's better to be out of equities and in defensive issues, or, for a more aggressive approach, to have a short position in equities.

During these overall trends, there will be counter moves. In every sustained rally there are periods of time when the market sells off, either as a short-term reaction to news, or as profits are being taken. Nonetheless, the market will follow the longer-term direction until a new trend is established. For example, from 1995 through 2000, the U.S. saw a period of strong economic growth, good employment and higher stock prices. Taking a long position in equities during that time would have yielded excellent results—although not without some pullbacks and declines due to a variety of factors and events. They included the Long-Term Capital Management hedge-fund debacle, the Russian debt default, and the currency crisis. The geopolitical and economic upheavals, however, proved to be short-term bumps, and the market found footing each time and continued to move higher. Had these same events occurred during a contracting economy, however, they would have most likely added to the downward momentum of the market, exacerbating a steady decline in stock prices.

ECONOMY AT A GLANCE

Economic Expansion
- **GDP**—Sequential quarterly growth starting at a rate of 3.75% or better.
- **Employment**—Average monthly job growth of 125,000, sustained over a quarter.
- **Stock Market**—Continual quarterly appreciation at a 9-10% annualized growth rate.

Economic Contraction
- **GDP**—Average quarterly growth rate below 3%, or sequential lower rates.
- **Employment**— Job losses over 3 or more months.
- **Stock Market**— Annualized growth rate below risk-free rate of interest (currently 4.25%), for several quarters.

As another example, the economy had begun to contract by the third quarter of 2000. The economy, by this point, was overbuilt, over-invested, over-expanded and over-stimulated. The peak had been reached, and the economy was beginning to decline. A year later, the tragedy of September 11, 2001, shocked the nation, but it did not cause the stock market's decline. Rather, these events occurred during a contraction, which pushed a falling market down farther, and faster. That also explains why it took so long for the market to recover. Economic factors and market forces were already impacting the market.

Against the backdrop of the overall trend, events occur that will either cause a momentary correction—to the upside or the downside —or that will add to the momentum in the prevailing direction. The challenge then becomes to discern the trend—despite outside forces—particularly at moments when the data is unclear, or an economic change has been detected. To do that, investment professionals should make a habit of studying economic data—month-to-month and quarter-to-quarter—in order to ascertain if the prevailing economic trend is still intact, or if the trend is beginning to change. Here are some examples from recent history to illustrate.

Q1 2000

A roaring economy and long bull run in the stock market made many people wonder if we'd ever see a bear market again. By Q1 2000, however, what were GDP, employment and the stock market saying about the economy? Let's take a look at the data from that time.

GDP*

Q1 2000	+1.0%
Q4 1999	+7.3%

Employment Situation — Change in Non-Farm Payrolls**

January 2000	February 2000	March 2000
+194,000	+146,000	+493,0000

Stock Market *(as measured by the monthly close for the Dow)*

March 2000	close 10,921.90
December 1999	close 11,497.12

The statistic that jumped out was the slowing in the rate of economic growth as evidenced by the drop in GDP from 7.3% in Q4 1999 to 1.0% in Q1 2000. Employment statistics, however, continued to increase, with more and more jobs added — including a strong 493,000 increase in March 2000. The stock market, as measured by the Dow's performance, did decline from the end of Q4 1999 to the end of Q1 2000. Would the GDP statistic alone prompt an investment decision? Probably not. But you would be on the alert to for the next quarter's economic performance.

Q2 2000

Let's take a look at what Q2 2000 statistics revealed:

GDP*

Q2 2000	+6.4%
Q1 2000	+1.0%

Employment Situation — Change in Non-Farm Payrolls**

April 2000	May 2000	June 2000
+308,000	+231,000	-25,000

Stock Market *(as measured by the monthly close for the Dow)*

June 2000	close 10,447.90
March 2000	close 10,921.90

The economic growth rate, as evidenced by GDP, picked up in Q2 2000 compared with the Q1. Employment statistics, however, began to tell a different story. Job creation slowed in April and May, and jobs were lost in June. This would raise an essential question: What was happening to the additional output, as measured by GDP? Obviously, inventories were built, but with payrolls not increasing, who would buy the additional goods? Further, how would GDP increase in the next quarter with fewer workers? The stock-market performance, meanwhile, was off somewhat, although not to any great degree. This is clearly a mixed economic picture, one that would raise a caution flag, which it did.

With the benefit of hindsight, we know that the economy did hit a peak and begin to contract in mid-2000. GDP growth was largely due to inventory building, although the stock market did not reflect the beginning of an economic contraction at this point. The loss of jobs, however, proved to be the first sign that the long, long run of economic growth was coming to an end.

Q3 2000

Let's move to the third quarter.

GDP*

Q3 2000	-0.5%
Q2 2000	+6.4%

Employment Situation—Change in Non-Farm Payrolls**

July 2000	August 2000	September 2000
+160,000	-28,000	+89,000

Stock Market *(as measured by the monthly close for the Dow)*

September 2000	close 10,650.90
June 2000	close 10,447.90

GDP showing a negative rate was a big signal of concern. Although some jobs were added, we know from previous experience that cuts in the labor force follow reduction in output. With GDP slowing dramatically, particularly compared with strong previous quarters, it seemed the long wave of upward momentum in the market and the economy was over. Astor made the determination in September 2000 that it was time to get out of long equity positions and to begin establishing a short position.

The economic slowdown was evident again in Q4 2000 with a GDP growth rate of only +2.1%. By Q1 2001, the contraction was clearly visible. GDP for that quarter came in at -0.2%, followed by readings of -0.6% in Q2 2001, and -1.3% in Q3 2001. By classic definition, a recession is two quarters of negative GDP readings. As for employment, payroll losses were recorded in 11 out of 12 months in 2001, with the steepest cuts coming in the second half of the year. And as for the stock market, the Dow closed March 2001 at 9,878.80, recovered by the end of June to 10,502,40, but finished September at 8,847.60, which also reflected the emotional and financial impact of the September 11th tragedy.

The downturn that began in the summer of 2000 continued into 2003. The overall direction of the economy was downward, although not without periods of market rallies. These upward surges in the market were the result of economic stimuli, including ultra-low interest rates that created a flood of "cheap" money, some of which found its way into the equities market. In addition, oversold conditions encouraged bargain hunters to begin venturing into the equities market, even though the economy had not turned from contraction to expansion.

> **These rallies during the downturn were the mirror opposite of the corrections we saw during the market's long expansion. Countertrend moves are to be expected, although the size and duration will depend upon the strength of the prevailing trend.**

These rallies during the downturn were the mirror opposite of the corrections we saw during the market's long expansion. Countertrend moves are to be expected, although the size and duration will depend upon the strength of the prevailing trend. Early on in the contraction, the market's interim rallies—moves that brought the market up 6%, 8% or even 10%—proved to be a small concern for the bears, just as corrections of that magnitude were of little consequence to the bulls during the market rally of the 1990s.

Then in 2003, the picture became mixed. We saw the first evidence that the stock market was diverging from economic performance. As discussed earlier in this chapter, the strength in the stock market was seen first in the Nasdaq, and later on, in the summer, in the S&P 500. Although a sustained economic improvement, particularly in the employment picture, had not been detected as yet, the stock market was acting as a leading indicator that the cycle had turned from contraction to expansion. Let's take a look at the data from mid-2003.

Q2 2003

GDP*

Q2 2003	+3.1%
Q1 2003	+2.0%

Employment Situation — Change in Non-Farm Payrolls**

April 2003	May 2003	June 2003
-20,000	-28,000	-14,000

Stock Market *(as measured by the monthly close for the Dow)*

June 2003	close 8,985.44
March 2003	close 7,992.13

As the statistics for Q2 2003 show, the GDP growth rate improved modestly. More troubling was the fact that the economy continued to lose jobs, although not nearly at the pace of previous months. Had we hit rock bottom? Despite this uncertain economic picture, the strength of the stock market couldn't be denied. The Dow closed Q2 2003 near the 9,000-mark, and money inflows continued to push prices higher.

This is a classic case of keeping an open mind when the economic picture is mixed. Despite concerns over the employment picture, an investor couldn't ignore the stock market. The more conservative approach at the time would have been to stay in cash until an economic expansion was confirmed. The more speculative investor might have taken a small position in equities, looking to participate in the early stages of the upside. In either case, it was clear that change was afoot and any position—from cash to a small equity position—had to be watched carefully. If the economy continued to improve, the cash-only investor would have wanted to get into the market, while the investor holding a small equities stake would want to add to that position.

Q3 2003

In Q3 2003, the picture became much clearer, with stronger growth in GDP and an improving employment scenario.

GDP*

Q3 2003	+8.2%
Q2 2003	+3.1%

Employment Situation—Change in Non-Farm Payrolls**

July	August	September
-45,000	-25,000	+67,000

Stock Market *(as measured by the monthly close for the Dow)*

September 2003	close 9,275.00
June 2003	close 8,985.44

The long-awaited economic recovery was confirmed, as more positive signs followed—including another 126,000 jobs added in October.

Economics in Action

Economic statistics are dynamic. Not only do they change from month to month, and quarter to quarter, they also ebb and flow with the pulse of U.S. business and the market. You don't have to be an economist to decipher economic statistics. Reading, understanding and tracking a few key statistics over a period of time will yield insights into how the economy is performing, what the prevailing trend is, and if the trend is changing. With this insight, investment professionals can help their clients make better and more informed decisions, with greater confidence, as part of an overall strategic plan.

The statistics on pages 59, 60, 62 & 63 were taken from the following sourcs:
***GPD:** Bureau of Economic Statistics
****Employment Situation—Change in Non-Farm Payrolls:** Bureau of Labor Statistics

Chapter 3

RISK, REWARD AND TRUE DIVERSIFICATION

If you said the word "diversification" to most retail investors, what would come to their minds? The first response would likely be that diversification is achieved by holding a certain percentage of assets in stocks, and a certain percentage in fixed income. Or they might take it a step further, suggesting that to diversify within an asset class, such as stocks, you need to hold a variety of equities: large caps, small caps, mid caps, growth and value, etc.

While these beliefs are widely held among retail investors, they are not examples of true diversification. To use a simple analogy, it's like filling up a dish with a scoop of vanilla ice cream, another of chocolate, a third of strawberry, and a fourth of pistachio, and maybe a few scoops of rocky road and mint-chocolate chip. It

> **As investment professionals and savvy investors know all too well, holding different kinds of stock will not provide true diversification, particularly in market downturns.**

may look and taste different, but it's still ice cream, and you haven't achieved a balanced diet, just by mixing up the colors on your plate. (And if you leave it out too long, it will all melt into the same indistinguishable mess.)

Similarly, as investment professionals and savvy investors know all too well, holding different kinds of stock will not provide true diversification, particularly in market downturns. In a bear market, some stocks will be quicker to fall than others. For example, the small-cap growth stocks may get hit first, while the more conservative large-cap value issues hold up a little better. But in time, most equities will go down. The only variation is the degree to which they decline. So, if one type of stock goes down 10%, another declines 25%, and yet another drops down 50%, is that diversification within equities? I don't think so.

One way to achieve true diversification within equities (or any other asset class for that matter) is through an active management approach. With an active management approach to equities, investors can buy (go long) when economic indicators point to an expansion and the stock market is rising. Conversely, investors can sell to exit long positions in equities (or even go short) when economic indicators point to a contraction, and the stock market is falling.

ECONOMICS BASED — ACTIVE MANAGEMENT

- **Economic Expansion** — Favors buying equities (long).
- **Economic Contraction** — Favors selling equities (taking profits or establishing short position), increasing cash and fixed income.
- **Long or Short** — Broad markets exposure through ETFs or Mutual Funds that replicate major indices — S&P and Nasdaq 100.

Through this long/short active management strategy, true diversification is achieved. While I believe economic indicators provide a valuable tool to rebalance your portfolio, many other indicators work as well. The most important thing to remember is that active management is the best way to truly diversify.

In this chapter, I will review a few scenarios in which active management plays a part. But first, I want to emphasize that it is not the role of the asset manager — the professional who is actively managing a portfolio — to determine an individual's risk tolerance and market exposure. That decision is best made by the client, with input from his or her investment advisor (asset gatherer).

Working with investment advisors and their clients, the only differentiations I make when deploying an active management strategy, are the amount of time an individual has been invested with us, and how far the economy is into the prevailing cycle. Otherwise, the risk determination and allocation of assets is between the client and the advisor, based on factors such as an investor's age, investment time horizon, earnings power, overall holdings, and risk tolerance.

For example, if a client has no appetite for risk, as evidenced from a large percentage holding of fixed-income assets, this individual is not a good candidate for an active management strategy for his or her equity holdings. If equities were a small percentage of the overall portfolio—say 25% to 30%—then the active management portion of those holdings would be similarly confined to a small percentage, perhaps 12% to 15%.

Now, let's take the case of someone who has a moderate risk tolerance, with roughly half his or her portfolio in equities, and half in fixed income. In this scenario, we would recommend that at least half of their equity assets (or 25% of the overall portfolio) be invested in an active management program. This approach, I believe, significantly reduces the risk of the long-only equity portion of the portfolio during market downturns. Moreover, this approach also increases the potential return over time.

To illustrate this point, consider this scenario: Investor A holds 100 percent of her portfolio in equities. If the market declines by 10 percent over time, the equity holdings would also be down about 10 percent (plus or minus a few percent, depending upon the performance of the individual stocks in her portfolio). However, if half the portfolio were invested using an active management approach, then sometime during the market's decline Investor A would have at least exited the market. Or, if Investor A's risk tolerance allowed it, she would be short the market with half of her overall equity holdings. Thus, during the downturn, her losses are at least cut in half from where they would be if she continued to hold equities. With a short position, she could reap profits during a downturn that would offset the losses on her equities, possibly to the extent that she broke even or made a small profit. In the worst-case scenario, she would have a smaller drawdown than with full equity exposure, and in the best case she would post a modest profit.

Now, when the market turns and begins to recover, Investor A can fully invest in equities again. But instead of having to make up for a 10 percent decline in her entire portfolio, Investor A is starting off with a small loss, a breakeven position, or a small profit. When the expanding market causes the stocks held in her portfolio to appreciate in value, Investor A reaps a larger return over time—and, more importantly, with reduced risk.

Model Portfolios

With this understanding, let's take a look at some hypothetical investor scenarios, and how active management could be used to reduce risk and enhance returns. In each instance the risk-tolerance determination—from a portfolio-management perspective—is based upon the percentage of equities held in an individual investor's portfolio.

Jonathan, a 36-year-old professional, is an aggressive investor whose portfolio is 90% invested in equities. Given his equity exposure and risk tolerance, Jonathan hopes to make large gains during a bull market. During market downturns, however, Jonathan stands potentially to lose a significant portion of the worth of his portfolio. This is the underlying problem with equity portfolios. The inevitable downturns in the stock market often occur when an equity-based portfolio is at the peak of its worth. Investors whose holdings were predominately in equities in 2001 will remember all too well the impact on their own portfolios.

For Jonathan, with 90% equity holdings, the investment recommendation would be for about half of these holdings to be actively managed. Specifically, I would recommend that 50% to 60% of his equity holdings be managed with a long/short strategy. The essence of the long-short strategy, as described in Chapter 2, is to be long equities when the economic indicators confirm an expansion, and to be short equities during a contraction.

Let's take a look at Jonathan's portfolio during each stage of the economic/business cycle.

Expansion Mode—Jonathan's Portfolio:

During economic expansion—as evidenced by growth in the GDP rate, relatively low unemployment, and an appreciating stock market—Jonathan will be heavily invested in equities. In keeping with his risk tolerance and investment temperament, during an expansion Jonathan's holdings will be 90% equities, but in a very specific mix:

Jonathan's Model Portfolio – Expansion Phase	
Total Equity Holdings	Total Fixed-Income and Cash Equivalents
90%	10%
40%-Individual Stocks	
50%-Active Management Equity (Indices) Holdings	

To reap the benefits of broad exposure to the stock market during an economic expansion, 50% of his equity holdings will be actively managed using exchange traded funds (ETFs) or mutual funds that replicate exposure to specific indices. Specifically, these instruments will provide exposure to the S&P 500 and Nasdaq 100.

Even though Jonathan is an aggressive investor with 90% of his overall holdings in equities, we would not recommend more than 50% to 60% of those holdings being actively managed. **The prime consideration is to use active management as a strategy to meaningfully diversify a portfolio, not to dominate or overwhelm it. Through active management, his equity holdings can be enhanced, while offering profit protection and opportunities to reap further gains during market contractions.**

For an aggressive investor such as Jonathan, another component of active management may also be included. A portion of his actively managed investment will be deployed in a momentum and trend-following system. This ac-

> The prime consideration is to use active management as a strategy to meaningfully diversify a portfolio, not to dominate or overwhelm it.

tive entry/exit strategy would allow Jonathan to benefit from opportunities—both short and long—that occur during the prevailing trend.

The objective of the active entry/exit strategy is to buy and sell, depending upon momentum and trend indicators, to take advantage of relatively short-term market moves. By capturing these moves, which occur frequently within a longer-term trend, returns can be further enhanced and risk can be reduced.

Several indicators can be used as part of the active entry/exit strategy. One option is a moving-average crossover, specifically tracking the market's positions relative to a moving average such as the 50-day, 100-day or 200-day. When the market crosses below the moving average, it signals a sell; when the market crosses above the moving average, it signals a buy. Or, a relative strength indicator can be used to determine the underlying strength (buy signal) or weakness (sell signal) in the market. At Astor, we use a ranking system that determines the number of up days (higher closes) or down days (lower closes) in a period. Based upon the prevailing trend of higher or lower closes, we enter or exit the market accordingly. We look for momentum signals in the direction of the economic trend to increase exposure and momentum signals to the contrary to reduce position size. Rarely will we completely change position direction from long to short (or vice versa) based solely on momentum.

> **The objective of the active entry/exit strategy is to buy and sell, depending upon momentum and trend indicators, to take advantage of relatively short-term market moves.**

Whatever indicators are used, the most important consideration is to be disciplined in this approach, and use only a portion of the actively managed assets. That way, even if a short-term directional move is missed, the majority of the assets that are actively managed remain invested according to the longer-term economic trend.

To illustrate how the positioning of Jonathan's portfolio would work, let's assume that now the economy starts to deteriorate. Long positions in the actively managed portion of his equity portfolio (50% of these holdings) would be exited. If the market dropped 20%, the net loss on Jonathan's portfolio would be 10%, reflecting the remainder of his equity position held in individual stocks. Over time, as economic conditions rebounded, long positions would be re-established with the portion that was sold. At this point, assume that the market rebounds by just 5%. That would be enough to get Jonathan's holdings back to flat.

> Whatever indicators are used, the most important consideration is to be disciplined in this approach, and use only a portion of the actively managed assets.

By contrast, a buy-and-hold investor would have been down 20% at the bottom of the market's decline, and after a 5% rebound would still be down 15%. Not only does Jonathan end up with a net profit, compared with a loss for the buy-and-hold investor, he does so with fewer of what I call "ulcer points." In other words, by actively managing his portfolio he can reduce risk in adverse market conditions easily and efficiently, while reaping the rewards of following the market trends, as defined by economic data. Similar results can also be achieved by actively managing assets in other markets as well, including fixed income, from both a short and long perspective.

Contraction Mode — Jonathan's Portfolio:

During an economic contraction — as evidenced by a decline in the GDP rate, increasing unemployment, and a decline in the stock market — active management would seek to protect Jonathan's gains that were reaped during the expansion phase. Beyond taking profits and selling a portion of his equity holdings, active management would also seek to profit through short positions during the contraction. This is achieved by either outright short sales in ETFs or the purchase of mutual funds that create inverse exposure to various market indices. For example, Rydex's Ursa Fund performs the opposite of the S&P 500 or Profunds' Short 500 Fund achieves that same investment objective.

Outside of the actively managed portion of the portfolio, Jonathan and his investment advisor could also decide to sell some individual stocks and increase his fixed-income and cash-equivalent holdings. For the sake of this illustration, we'll assume that Jonathan decides to reduce his individual stock holdings and increase his fixed income/cash equivalents as shown below. His actively managed portion, however, remains approximately 50% of his previous overall equity holdings.

Jonathan's Model Portfolio — Contraction Phase

Total Equity Holdings	Total Fixed-Income and Cash Equivalents
90% (Before Adjustment)	10%
20% - Individual Stocks	30%
50% - Active Management Equity Holdings	

Once again, the actively managed portion of his equity holdings would utilize ETFs to establish a short position in the indices. Or, mutual funds that offer the equivalent of a short position in the market can be used. Through these inverse funds, when an index declines, the value of the fund increases by the same amount. The objective of active management during the contraction is two-fold. For one, it lessens Jonathan's long equity exposure during the unfavorable market conditions associated with a contraction. More importantly, it also seeks to reap profits from the falling market, which could at least offset any losses Jonathan incurs elsewhere in his portfolio. Potentially, if his short position is sizeable enough, and the market decline is significant, Jonathan could make a net profit on his overall holdings.

In addition, the active entry/exit strategy would be utilized to capitalize on short-term momentum and trend opportunities. Again, this would involve about 20% of Jonathan's actively managed holdings.

The objective would be to look for opportunities to buy the market to take advantage of short-term upward, countertrend moves that occur during contractions and to sell when move is over.

Throughout the management of Jonathan's holdings, the strategies deployed are matched with his investment objectives, time frame and risk tolerance. This is far better than determining an individual's holdings based upon age, which assumes that every 30-year-old, 50-year-old or 70-year-old has the same risk tolerance and time frame. There could be very conservative, risk-averse 30-year-olds for whom active management should be deployed conservatively—if at all. Or, there could be highly risk tolerant 70-year-olds for whom active management would be an ideal strategy. Once again, it is the role of the investment advisor, who knows the clients best, to advise them.

Monica, a 59-year-old widow with two grown children, is a moderate-risk investor. She has roughly half of her holdings in equities and half in fixed-income/cash equivalents. Her investment objectives are to preserve capital while also growing her portfolio steadily over time. Active management within her equity holdings will help further these goals.

Expansion Mode — Monica's Portfolio:

During economic expansion, Monica's overall holdings will reflect her 50-50 split. However, the equity portion will be divided between individual stocks and active management holdings, using a long/short strategy.

Monica's Model Portfolio — Expansion Phase	
Total Equity Holdings	Total Fixed-Income and Cash Equivalents
50%	50%
25% - Individual Stocks	
25% - Active-Management Equity Holdings	

As in the previous example, the actively managed portion will utilize ETFs or mutual funds to replicate long exposure to the S&P 500 and Nasdaq 100. Although Monica is a moderate-risk investor, we would not recommend less than 50% of her equity holdings be deployed using active management, representing 25% of her overall portfolio.

If a smaller percentage were committed to active management, the overall diversification effect would be greatly diluted.

Using a long/short strategy, Monica would have long exposure to the major indices when the economic data indicated the expansion was continuing. Because of her overall moderate-risk tolerance and her need for capital preservation, the more aggressive, active entry/exit strategy would not be deployed.

Contraction Mode — Monica's Portfolio:

During economic contraction, Monica's equity position could remain 50% of her portfolio, or a slightly smaller percentage if she and her investment advisor decide to sell some individual stocks in her portfolio. Nonetheless, 25% of her portfolio would remain actively managed. In this scenario, a slight adjustment of her equity holdings is assumed.

Monica's Model Portfolio — Contraction Phase	
Total Equity Holdings	Total Fixed-Income and Cash Equivalents
45%	55%
20% - Individual Stocks	
25% - Active Management Equity Holdings	

Using the long/short strategy for her actively managed holdings, short positions would be established using ETFs or mutual funds as soon as an economic contraction was detected and confirmed. Throughout the economic contraction, this portion of her portfolio would remain short, to capitalize on the overall downtrend. The goal would be to offset losses incurred from her other equity holdings, thus preserving capital and providing a better foundation for the future when the economy turned and expansion resumed.

While active management can be deployed to reduce risk and potentially improve returns, it is not for every investor. For example, Donald and Sylvia are in their mid-50s. Their portfolio is held mostly in 401(k) and other retirement holdings. They are conservative investors with about 70% of their holdings in fixed-income and cash equivalents, and 30% in equities, mostly mutual funds. Given their low-risk tolerance, active management would not be an appropriate strategy for them. In fact, an investment professional who knows this couple and their risk tolerance would not even present the active management strategy to them.

As these model portfolios illustrate, true asset diversification can maximize returns, and minimize overall risk, by taking advantage of opportunities presented in rising *and* falling markets. Most importantly, the strategies must be tailored to the individual's investment objectives and risk tolerance. In fact, that is the beauty of active management. When the right portion of a portfolio is committed to an active management strategy, an investor can protect against adverse market moves without putting too much of their holdings at risk. Active management is a powerful strategy that belongs in many investors' portfolios. The key is for investors to work with their advisors to determine the right portfolio mix to match their risk profile, while reaching their objectives for growth and capital preservation. For those who chose active management, the next determination is to find a portfolio manager whose strategies and programs meet their criteria and expectations.

Chapter 4

ACTIVE MANAGEMENT — A CASE STUDY

O ver the last century, the simple act of investing has grown from an exclusive VIP dinner to an all you can eat buffet. Access to information and self-investing has given individuals with $250 or more the ability to create an investment portfolio. Research that used to be limited to Wall Street is now available on Main Street, at the click of a mouse. However, portfolios still require a proper approach to achieve financial goals and to limit risk. Asset allocation has evolved to enable investors to survive the "swings." In this chapter, using a hypothetical portfolio, we will demonstrate the value of using these new investment allocation strategies.

Background

Back in the late 19th century through the turn of the twentieth, investing was not available to 95% of the public. The Vanderbilts, the Rockefellers and folks in high society were the owners of wealth, able to stake ownership in whatever they pleased. As our country moved toward the Depression, little changed. The Great Depression went on to decimate the net worth of many. However, it was not the stock market crash alone that took away wealth, as few common people actually owned stock. It was the economy that crumbled, eliminating jobs (with that income) and decreasing the quality of life.

After recovering from a lengthy depression, the U.S. enjoyed an equally long expansion. It then became clear that the market and the economy moved in cycles. Within these identifiable cycles, certain assets performed better than others. While access to stocks and stockbrokers was expensive, it was clear that buying stocks, at certain times, was a good thing. This brought about a new problem: risk. Investing in just a few stocks left you exposed to the risk of having one or all of those companies fail to perform. In the context of these two points, there had to be an easier method to invest in a diversified manner in these asset classes without incurring such steep costs. This gave birth to the mutual fund. These pre-selected groups of companies were an efficient way for investors of all sizes to diversify their holdings within this asset class and thus continue on the path of broad based equity ownership.

Enter in the 90s. An economic boom like we had never seen began to take shape. As the technology age progressed, so did the availability of information on which to base your investment decisions. The ease of obtaining this information, the 24-hour chat rooms and the venture capital money that poured on entrepreneurs at a pace that eventually proved unsustainable (and unsubstantiated), were keys to proliferating a permanent change in investor mentality and participation. Every Joe and Susan became a market expert, willing to accept greater risk for what appeared to be unlimited return. When stocks are only going up across the board, it's hard to be wrong. The phrase "new paradigm" was the rallying cry of this new age of investing. While the chat rooms soon died down and dollars to entrepreneurs who simply posed a glimmer of an idea (not to mention no profits) soon dried up, the information and the speed of access was changed forever.

Eventually, the exuberance ended as we realized that profits and valuations do matter. Markets do not go up forever, and the ones that go up fast come down even faster. Losses amounting from 50-80% were common. Thousands of paper millionaires saw their "net worth" go up in smoke. This was our reminder that the economic and market cycles were alive and well, and not to be treated lightly.

To illustrate how far and widespread investing had come, stock market crashes/economic recessions had not successfully decreased average household wealth until the 2000-2002 market pull-back. Even mutual fund ownership, which is supposed to help diversify your portfolio, was unable to curtail the decrease your portfolio saw during that period. With household wealth now so tied to the stock market, it has become imperative for asset allocation to evolve even further to address these situations.

Limitations of Buy-and-Hold Investing

Historic returns in the stock market have averaged about 9.76% per year from 1886-2001, according to Jeremy Siegel, author of *Stocks for the Long Run* (p. 293). That's a nice annual return if you can realize it. (Most funds actually under perform their benchmark indexes on a regular basis.) However, buy-and-hold has an inherent problem as a standalone strategy. If stated that while achieving a 9.76% return you would see your capital decline by 30-60%, that would paint a little different picture. That average return of 9.76% includes these market pullbacks, which naturally occur when you have the largest exposure to the markets. Further as fate would have it your portfolio will decline when you think you need your money most.

We are, by nature, emotional, and sitting through these stomach-churning markets is a very difficult thing to do. In fact, most investors end up selling near the bottom and do not end up getting back in until the market has well passed their exit point on the way back up. With that action alone, you miss a significant portion of the market's return and need to work even harder to get it back. In other words, you have to sit through a 30-60% pullback only to achieve a long-run average return of less than 10%! (If you did indeed sit through it.) Keep in mind the 9.76% is a simple arithmetic average return. Actual returns, geometrically stated (taking into account compounding), will be significantly less.

Many investors do end up holding through the ups and downs attempting to weather the storm because they have a longer time horizon for their financial needs. What would happen if one of those financial needs occurred sooner than expected, or something came up and you needed money now? If that need came in the middle, or worse yet at the bottom of a drawdown, (*see* years 7 or 8 in Chart 4-1), how devastating could that be? Aside from the financial need to make up a greater portion of those assets, it also reduces the capital base from which to compound your returns during the next positive period.

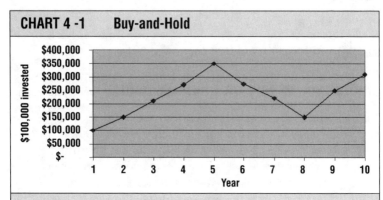

CHART 4-1 Buy-and-Hold

By definition your financial needs become more urgent when the value of your financial assets have declined. Unexpected financial needs that may come during drawdowns (years 7 and 8) make buy-and-hold a risky proposition.

What's missing in most investment portfolios is a strategy that smoothes out the impact of adverse market conditions. Now take that same "financial needs" scenario stated previously. What if there were a value-added strategy that could limit your drawdowns without sacrificing your upside potential? Think of the benefits of a portfolio that looked like the one in Chart 4-2. This value-added strategy is called **active management**. In this scenario, you would have a much eas-

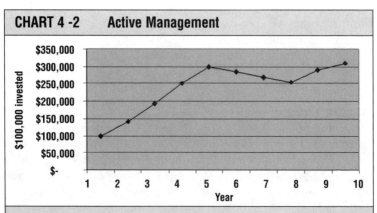

CHART 4-2 Active Management

By limiting the drawdowns, your financial decisions can be made on your own terms, not the market's. Furthermore, you need less time with less risk to make up profits from adverse market moves.

ier time (and less worry) meeting financial demands in years 7 and 8. The bottom line is that **you can make your financial decisions on your own terms, not the market's terms.**

When the economy is doing well, you can make money by investing in almost any sector. That's not where the value is. When the economy is doing poorly, you can lose money in almost any sector. A strategy that sees this and positions you to limit the losses; **now that is value!** This strategy, by definition, is called **active management.**

What Is Active Management?

Active management means taking a proactive approach to investing by utilizing fundamental and/or technical analysis, to create value in a portfolio beyond that of buy-and-hold. It is, simply, the antithesis of buy-and-hold investing.

As a result of the situations in the market even over the recent three decades, we realized there were things that had to be done in order to mitigate losses in adverse markets and even create profitable opportunities in bear markets. (Yes, they do exist.) The objective of this case study is to demonstrate the value to a portfolio of active management in general, of which there are many different styles. Astor follows one style in particular: economic cycle analysis.

As stated in previous chapters, the economy has cycles (expansion, peak, contraction and trough), just like a year has seasons. Throughout the economic cycles, the market goes up and goes down. The key is to address these cycles and add value to a portfolio by providing strategies that work in all market conditions. At Astor Asset Management, we have developed strategies that position client portfolios to profit in both up and down markets, through all the aforementioned cycles. Our programs work to diversify your portfolio so the drawdowns you see in down markets are not as deep, while still helping your account to grow in up markets. You no longer have to be held hostage by a "buy-and-hope" strategy or by natural economic cycles.

A New Asset Class

To further illustrate the purpose of diversification with an active management strategy such as Astor, we have created a hypotheti-

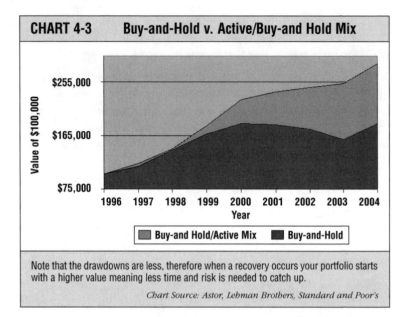

CHART 4-3   Buy-and-Hold v. Active/Buy-and Hold Mix

Value of $100,000

$255,000

$165,000

$75,000

1996 1997 1998 1999 2000 2001 2002 2003 2004
Year

■ Buy-and Hold/Active Mix   ■ Buy-and-Hold

Note that the drawdowns are less, therefore when a recovery occurs your portfolio starts with a higher value meaning less time and risk is needed to catch up.

Chart Source: Astor, Lehman Brothers, Standard and Poor's

cal portfolio containing just stocks and bond in the prior eight years. We then compared that to what that same portfolio may have looked like had you mixed an actively managed approach like Astor with your portfolio during that same time period.

In Chart 4-3, the buy-and-hold portfolio (dark shade) contained a 60% allocation to the S&P 500[1] and a 40% allocation to the Lehman Brothers Aggregate Bond Index[2], a moderately conservative portfolio. The active/buy-and-hold mix (light shade) was comprised of 50% of the buy-and-hold and 50% of the Astor Balanced program.

The active/buy-and-hold mix was able to significantly outperform the straight buy-and-hold, as it was able to side step the decline and position the portfolio to garner returns during the economic contraction. As you can imagine, a more aggressive buy-and-hold portfolio (one containing higher beta stocks with less fixed income) would have seen more pronounced drawdowns from 2000 to 2002.

---

[1] The S&P Index is an unmanaged composite of 500 large capitalization companies.

[2] Lehman Brothers Aggregate Bond index is a composite return of a diverse range of U.S. debt instruments.

Risk and Reward

The greater the risk an investor is willing to take, the greater the potential reward they are going to require in return for that risk. Standard deviation is one measure of risk/volatility of a certain asset. (Treasury yields are labeled as risk-free assets because the risk of default/non-payment on the coupon and principal is minimal.) Generally speaking, in order to reduce risk, you end up sacrificing return. However, active management has the unique ability to reduce overall risk without reducing long-term returns. (*See* Chart 4-4)

CHART 4-4	Risk/Return Profiles					
	Buy-and-Hold		**Mix**		**Return to Risk Ratio**	
	Ret	Std. Dev.	Ret	Std. Dev.	Buy-and-Hold	Mix
1 Year	17.90%		13.16%			
3 Year	0.49%	14.73%	6.23%	5.91%	0.03	1.05
5 Year	2.19%	11.55%	9.50%	9.01%	0.19	1.05
8 Year	8.05%	12.28%	14.04%	9.78%	0.66	1.44

Reducing risk in a portfolio can be done easily. Doing so without compromising return is more difficult, but can be done through active management. The Active/Buy-and-Hold mix portfolio is actually able to increase return while decreasing risk. The return-to-risk ratios illustrate how much return (percent) you achieve per 1% of risk you carry in the portfolio. If your ratio is too far below 1, you are putting on too much risk for the return you are getting.

Chart Source: Astor, Lehman Brothers, Standard and Poor's

Why Should You Worry About Drawdowns?

One of the most important points when choosing an investment target is the amount of drawdown you will experience and how long it takes to recover.

- **Drawdown:** The total decrease (percentage or dollars) that your account falls from the highest peak value seen by the account.

- **Recovery:** How long it takes from the low value in the drawdown to get back to making new highs.

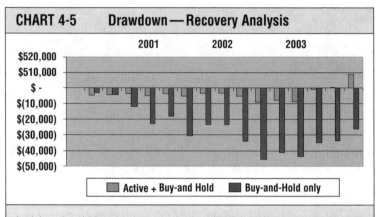

CHART 4-5   Drawdown — Recovery Analysis

Legend: ■ Active + Buy-and-Hold   ■ Buy-and-Hold only

Look how the addition of active management reduced the overall loss of the portfolio thus turning to profitability sooner than straight buy-and-hold. Even with the huge gains in the past 12 months, smaller gains over that same period combined with smaller losses (or even profits) during the adverse years have created a profitable portfolio.

Chart Source: Astor, Standard and Poor's

These are very important statistics because, generally speaking, the lower the drawdown, the shorter the recovery time. Conversely, the faster the recovery time, the larger the drawdown you will be willing to accept. (See Chart 4-5.)

If we have failed to drive the idea home at this point, consider the following: Hypothetically, if you invested your money in the same mixes (buy-and-hold vs. active/buy-and-hold mix) previously stated at the worst possible time (Q2 2000), that portfolio would have the following cumulative gains/losses during the corresponding quarters.

Your buy-and-hold portfolio, if mixed with active management, would have lost no more than $9,200, compared with a loss of $46,000 in an S&P 500 buy-and-hold position. Additionally, the active mix portfolio is already recovered and is up over $8,500 while the buy-and-hold portfolio is still down $25,000, even with a 30% plus return in 2003.

The Case Study

Chart 4-6 depicts a quarterly illustration of account value over time. The straight S&P 500 portfolio symbolizes the track of a buy-and-hold

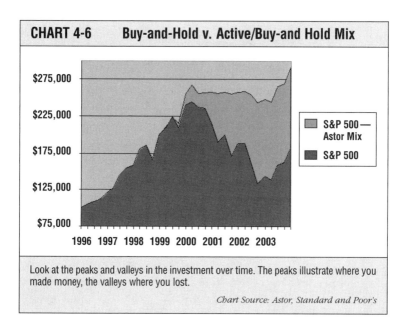

CHART 4-6   Buy-and-Hold v. Active/Buy-and Hold Mix

Legend:
- S&P 500 — Astor Mix
- S&P 500

Look at the peaks and valleys in the investment over time. The peaks illustrate where you made money, the valleys where you lost.

Chart Source: Astor, Standard and Poor's

strategy that correlated 100% with the S&P 500 (equity position only) over this time period. The mix is a combination of the Astor Balanced Program (50%) and the buy-and-hold S&P 500 (50%).

There are two significant declines the S&P 500 experienced from 1996-2000 during the bull market. In Q3 1998, the S&P was down 10.3%, while the active/buy-and-hold mix would have seen a 6.8% decline (saving you nearly 35% of the losses you would have incurred). Similarly, the S&P 500 fell 6.56% in Q3 1999, while the mix only declined 3.75% (saving you 43% of that loss). Again, with a significant reduction in volatility of your assets, you can feel more comfortable about making important financial decisions, and have a larger asset base to compound during positive market environments.

The major benefit of active management occurs during uncertain or changing market conditions. Significant evidence of this was exhibited during the following three years from 2000-2003. At the lowest point in the decline of the S&P 500, which occured in 2002, the index was down 45.6%. Compare that with a 9.2% decline by the active/buy-and-hold mix portfolio. During the worst three year period our financial markets have possibly ever seen, a mix of buy-and-hold with active management, specifically Astor, declined less than 10% at its lowest point, preserving the majority of your capital. Four quarters from the lowest point in the mix portfolio, your account was again making new highs. The buy-and-hold of the S&P 500, even with the 26% increase in 2003, still needs a 34% move (compounded) just to break the 2000 high. Imagine, if all of your money was in high-risk stocks such as the Nasdaq, you are still down 60%!

Conclusion

The deeper the declines in your portfolio, the greater the returns you will need in subsequent periods to restore the initial value of your portfolio. If a portfolio of $100,000 declines 50% to $50,000, you will need a 100% return from that point to recover the initial value. If you are able to cut that loss to just 25% to a lowest portfolio value of $75,000, that portfolio will need only a 33% return from that point to recover the initial value. All else being equal, the 33% return should take significantly less time to achieve than the 100%, based on the laws of positive compounding (which are

CHART 4-7 2000-2003 Portfolio Analysis	Buy-and-Hold	Active Mix
Beginning Investment (3/31/2000)	$100,000	$100,000
Lowest value of account during period	$54,410	$90,795
Largest yearly return during period (2003)	31%	19%
Quarters from low to complete recovery	5 and counting	4
Current Value (as of 12/31/2003)	$74,201	$108,569
Out-performance of buy-and-hold by mix	46%	

By limiting how far the portfolio value dropped, the active mix portfolio was able to utilize the powers of positive compounding to significantly outperform the buy-and-hold strategy by 46% in a 3.75-year period, even though it underperformed by 12 percentage points in 2003.

much more effective following limited drawdowns). We all know that *time* is one of the most important factors in investing that we can have on our side.

The point is clear. The mix of buy-and-hold and active management created a much more desirable effect in the long term. Through active management your portfolio drawdown was smaller, your recovery time was shorter, and as a result your overall returns were greater with much less risk.

Now that should make you sleep better at night!

Astor Asset Management is a Registered Investment Advisor with the U.S. Securities and Exchange Commission that specializes in separately managed accounts. All research and opinions contained herein is for informational purposes only. This is not a solicitation to offer investment advice or services.

Chapter 5

STRATEGIES FOR TOMORROW'S MARKETS

The market correction of 2000-2002 taught an important, albeit painful, lesson for investors—a lesson that we at Astor Asset Management have been teaching clients for years. Rather than put their hope (and money) on buy-and-hold, investors must recognize the need to take a more active approach to investing. To meet the needs of these sophisticated investors, investment professionals should offer more than just the mutual fund flavor of the month or hot stock pick. Savvy investors are looking for *strategies* that will serve them not only in today's market conditions, but tomorrow's as well.

To meet the needs of their clients, investment professionals need to understand the advantages of active management, which allows investment decisions to be made based on specific market and/or other criteria—such as Astor's strategy of economics-based active management.

Through active management, investors have the potential to improve returns and reduce risk. Moreover, they can bring true diversification to their portfolios to guard against downturns and improve returns in favorable conditions. This is vitally important in today's new investment climate of shorter, less defined cycles.

Bullish or bearish, economic expansion or contraction, the cycles will continue. Savvy investors and the investment professionals who advise them, should not be afraid when the cycles change. Through active management, they will be empowered to take bolder decisions which, over time, can improve returns while reducing unfavorable market exposure.

GLOSSARY OF
ECONOMIC TERMS

There are a variety of indicators that reflect at least one aspect of the U.S. economy. Some of the indicators are broad measurements, such as Gross Domestic Product (GDP), which gauges the output of U.S. business. Others, such as Vehicle Sales, have a far more limited scope. Taken together, the indicators provide in-depth information about how the economy has been performing and a hint of what is likely to come.

At Astor Asset Management, our economics-based approach to active management requires that we closely monitor economic data. While we give more weight to some indicators (such as GDP and the Employment Situation) over others, each report lends some meaning. The best way to make informed investment decisions is with a thorough understanding of the current state of the economy (expansion, peak, contraction, or trough) and the strength or weakness of that prevailing trend. We also believe that investment professionals and their savvy clientele should be familiar with economic reports and indicators, to understand their meaning and discern their relative importance.

Following is a glossary of economic reports, with a brief description of each. To view Astor's Economic Calendar, which is updated daily with the latest economic reports and indicators, visit the Astor web site at www.astorllc.com, and sign up for our free "Logical Economics" newsletter.

Beige Book

Commonly known as the Beige Book, the Federal Reserve's "Summary of Commentary on Current Economic Conditions" is published eight times a year. Each Federal Reserve Bank gathers anecdotal information on current economic conditions in its district through reports from bank and branch directors and interviews with key businessmen, economists, market experts, and other sources. The Beige Book outlines this information by district and sector. It does not represent the views of the Federal Reserve Board or the Federal Reserve Banks, but summarizes comments from businesses and contacts outside of the Federal Reserve System.

Business Inventories

This report from the Bureau of Census includes three components. Monthly Retail Trade presents data on dollar-value of retail sales and sales for selected establishment, as well as a sub-sample of firms providing data on end-of-month inventories. Monthly Wholesale Trade includes data on dollar values of merchant wholesalers' sales and end-of-month inventories. Manufacturers report current production levels and future production commitments, as well as the value of shipments, new orders net of cancellations, month-end total inventory, materials and supplies, work-in-process, and finished goods inventories.

Chain Store Sales (Mitsubishi Index)

The Mitsubishi Index is one of the longest running chain store indices. It tracks spending at major chain stores that fit in the broad general merchandise, apparel, and furniture category. The Mitsubishi Index includes only *same-store* sales (sales from stores that have been in business for at least a year). Because the index is a same-store sales index, retail industry expansion is not immediately captured in the index, and the result is that the Mitsubishi Index tends to underestimate sales growth. The index is reported as a percentage change from one year ago and covers the following specialized retail groupings: apparel, building supply, department, discount, drug, electronic, footwear, furniture, and wholesale clubs.

Chicago Fed National Activity Index

The Chicago Fed National Activity Index, released monthly by the Chicago Federal Reserve Board, is a coincident indicator of broad economic activity. An index reading of "zero" indicates that the economy is growing at its long-run potential growth rate. A value above zero indicates that the economy is growing above potential, while a negative value indicates that the economy is growing below potential. The index is a weighted average of 85 indicators of national economic activity. These indicators are drawn from 5 broad categories of data: (1) production and income; (2) employment, unemployment, and hours worked; (3) personal consumption and housing; (4) manufacturing and trade sales; (5) inventories and orders.

Conference Board's Consumer Confidence Survey

The Conference Boards' Consumer Confidence Survey measures the level of confidence that individual households have in the performance of the economy. Survey questionnaires are mailed to a nationwide representative sample of 5,000 households, of which approximately 3,500 respond. Households are asked five questions to rate the current business conditions in the household's area; business conditions six months into the future, job availability in the area, job availability in six months, and family income in six months. Responses are seasonally adjusted. An index is constructed for each response and then a composite index is fashioned based on the responses. Two other indices—one to assess the present situation and one for expectations about the future—are also constructed. Expectations account for 60 percent of the index, while the current situation is responsible for the remaining 40 percent.

Conference Board's Help Wanted Index

The Conference Board's Help Wanted Index surveys help-wanted advertising in 51 major newspapers across the nation. The Conference Board then constructs an index based on the volume of advertising. An index is created for the nation, covering the nine census divisions and for the 51 metro areas in which the newspapers are published. The base year is 1987, with a value of 100. The index is seasonally adjusted.

Conference Board's Leading Indicators

The Conference Board's Leading Indicators is a composite index constructed as a weighted average of 10 key economic data, designed to predict near-term economic conditions. The index generally turns down before a recession and turns up before an expansion. The indicators that comprise the index listed in order of importance are: spread between the 10-year Treasury and the Fed Funds rate, M2 money supply, average work week in manufacturing, manufacturers' new orders for consumer goods, S&P 500, average weekly initial unemployment claims, vendor performance component of the Institute for Supply Management (ISM) index, housing permits, consumer expectations, and manufacturers' new orders for nondefense capital goods.

Construction Spending

Construction Spending, from the Bureau of Census, reports the dollar value of newly completed structures. Individual data series are available for several residential building types; nonresidential private building types; public buildings, and other public and private structures, such as roads and utility lines. Both current dollar and inflation-adjusted estimates are available. This release is used directly to estimate the investment in the structures component of the expenditures estimate of GDP. Since a building is not recorded in the data series until it is completed, this series is a lagging indicator of construction activity.

Consumer Confidence Survey

See **Conference Board's Consumer Confidence Survey**.

Consumer Credit

Consumer Credit, from the Federal Reserve Board, represents loans for households for financing consumer purchases of goods and services, and for refinancing existing consumer debt. Secured and unsecured loans are included, except those secured with real estate (mortgages, home equity loans and lines, etc). Securitized consumer loans, loans made by finance companies, banks, and retailers that are sold as securities are included. The two categories of consumer credit are revolving and nonrevolving debt. Revolving debt covers credit card use whether for purchases or for cash advances, store charge accounts, and check credit plans that allow overdrafts up to certain amounts on personal accounts. It accounts for about 43 percent of consumer installment debt outstanding. The nonrevolving category was created in 1999 by combining the old categories "auto" and "other" and includes auto, personal, student, and other miscellaneous loans such as recreation vehicle loans.

Consumer Price Index (CPI)

The Consumer Price Index (CPI) is a measure of the average change over time in the prices paid by urban consumers for a fixed market basket of consumer goods and services. The CPI report, released by the Bureau of Labor Statistics, provides a way for consumers to compare what the market basket of goods and services costs this month with what the same market basket cost a month or a year ago. The CPI reports price changes in over 200 categories, arranged into eight major groups. The CPI includes various user fees such as water and sewerage charges, auto registration fees, vehicle tolls, and so forth. Taxes that are directly associated with the prices of specific goods and services (such as sales and excise taxes) are also included.

Consumer Sentiment Survey
See **University of Michigan Consumer Sentiment Survey**

Current Account

The Current Account report from the Bureau of Economic Analysis reflects the movement of non-capital items in the balance of payments account. The report breaks out the balance on goods, services, and income. Changes in the current account balance are a useful barometer for the state of U.S. foreign trade as well as the flow of investment to and from the United States. A widening deficit on the current account is typical when the United States is purchasing excessive imports. The current account also provides a good measure of the performance of the United States in the international markets.

Durable Goods

Durable Goods from the Bureau of the Census is the advance release of overall factory orders and shipments. Durable goods are industrial products with an expected life of 1 year or more. They include intermediate goods, such as steel, lumber, and electronic components; finished industrial machinery and equipment; and finished consumer durable goods, such as furniture, autos, and TVs. Data are reported for seven different industry groupings, plus the total. New orders are the dollar volume of orders for new products received by domestic manufacturers from any source, domestic or foreign.

ECRI Future Inflation Gauge (FIG)

The Economic Cycle Research Institute's (ECRI) future inflation gauge (FIG) is a weighted average of eight key economic data series designed to predict cyclical swings in the inflation rate. Components used to construct the index are: industrial materials prices, real estate loans, insured unemployment rate, yield spread, civilian employment, federal and nonfederal debt, import prices, and the percentage of purchasing managers reporting slower deliveries.

ECRI Weekly Leading Index

The Economic Cycle Research Institute's (ECRI) weekly leading index is a weighted average of seven key economic data created to predict economic conditions in the near term. Designed to be clearly cyclical, the index is constructed to turn down before a recession and turn up before an expansion.

Employment Cost Index

The Employment Cost Index (ECI) from the Bureau of Labor Statistics is based on a survey of employer payrolls taken in the third month of the quarter for the pay period including the 12th day of the month. The survey is a probability sample of approximately 3,600 private industry employers and 700 state and local governments, public schools, and public hospitals. The ECI measures changes in labor costs of money wages and salaries, and noncash fringe benefits in nonfarm private industry and state and local government.

Employment Situation

Payroll figures are reported each month by the Bureau of Labor Statistics in its employment situation report. Payroll employment is a measure of the number of jobs in more than 500 industries, except for farming, in all states and 255 metropolitan areas. The employment estimates are based on a survey of larger businesses. The report also provides information on average weekly hours worked and average hourly earnings, which are important indicators of the tightness of labor markets. An index of aggregate weekly hours worked is also included in the release, which gives an important early indication of production before the quarterly GDP numbers come out. An estimate of the labor force, employment, and unemployment is provided in a parallel survey of U.S. households.

Existing Home Sales

Each month the National Association of Realtors (NAR) Research Division receives data on existing single-family home sales from over 650 boards and associations of realtors and multiple listing systems across the country. This data is included in the Existing Home Sales Report.

Factory Orders

The Factory Orders report from the Bureau of the Census includes the dollar volume of new orders, shipments, unfilled orders, and inventories reported by domestic manufacturers. Data are reported for numerous industry groupings, plus the total and specialized aggregates. New orders are a good measure of demand for each industry and in aggregate, and shipments are a good measure of supply. Unfilled orders are the backlog of orders that have been received by domestic manufacturers, but not yet shipped. Unfilled orders are one indication of the balance between demand and supply, most often used to indicate an excess of demand relative to supply. Inventories are another key indicator of the relative trends of demand and supply, most often used to indicate an excess of supply over demand.

Federal Open Market Committee (FOMC) Meeting

The Federal Open Market Committee of the Federal Reserve Board (FOMC) meets approximately every 6 weeks to consider whether any changes need to be made to monetary policy. The FOMC is comprised of the seven Federal Reserve Board members, including the current chairman, and five Federal Reserve District Bank presidents.

FOMC Minutes

The minutes of each Federal Open Market Committee (FOMC) meeting are released a few days after the subsequent FOMC meeting. The minutes generally include a discussion of the economic and financial factors the FOMC considers when making a decision regarding the direction of monetary policy. The minutes also indicate whether the Fed has a bias toward future monetary tightening or easing.

Gross Domestic Product (GDP)

Gross Domestic Product (GDP) is a measure of the total production and consumption of goods and services in the United States. The report, released by the Bureau of Economic Analysis, includes two complementary measures of GDP, one based on income and one based on expenditures. GDP is measured one way by adding up the labor, capital, and tax costs of producing the output. On the consumption side, GDP is measured by adding up expenditures by households, businesses, government, and net foreign purchases. Theoretically, these two measures should be equal. However, due to problems collecting the data, there is often a discrepancy between the two measures. The GDP price deflator is used to convert output measured at current prices into constant-dollar GDP.

Help Wanted Index
See **Conference Board's Help Wanted Index**

Housing Starts and Building Permits
Released by the Census Bureau of the Department of Commerce, this report reflects residential construction activity in the U.S. The Housing Starts figure reflects the number of residential units on which construction has begun. The Building Permits portion reflects permits that are issued in order for excavation to begin. While Building Permits typically lead Housing Starts, permits are not required in every region of the country. Therefore, Housing Starts over time may be larger than Building Permits. The report is broken down by region: Northeast, Midwest, South, and West.

Import and Export Prices
Every month, the Bureau of Labor Statistics collects net transaction prices for more than 20,000 products from over 6,000 companies and secondary sources to formulate the Import and Export Prices report. The overall import price index measures the price change of products purchased from other countries by U.S. residents. The overall export price index measures the change in the prices of domestically produced U.S. goods shipped to other countries. These prices are then weighted according to the relative importance (i.e., the share of expenditures) of the product in 1995.

Industrial Production/Capacity Utilization
The Industrial Production index, released by the Federal Reserve Board, measures the change in output in U.S. manufacturing, mining, and electric and gas utilities. Output refers to the physical quantity of items produced. The index covers the production of goods and power for domestic sales in the United States and for export. It excludes production in the agriculture, construction, transportation, communication, trade, finance, and service industries; government output and imports. Then, each component is weighted according to its relative importance in the base period. The report also includes

Capacity Utilization, which gauges how much available "capacity" exists. The greater the capacity utilization, the higher the production level, which could indicate inflation (typically a measurement over the 85% mark). Conversely, a low capacity number indicates economic weakness as industries are producing below their potential.

Initial Jobless Claims

This weekly report from the Department of Labor measures the number of applicants filing for state jobless benefits. The report is important as an indicator of employment and, therefore, economic trends. An increase in jobless claims, for example, shows that job prospects are worsening (or at least have not improved), while a decrease in claims indicates job growth. On a week-to-week basis, the claims number can be volatile. Therefore, looking at jobless claims over a longer time period (such as month-to-month) may be more meaningful.

International Trade

The International Trade report from the Department of Commerce reflects the balance of trade, or the difference between exports and imports of goods and services. Merchandise data are provided for U.S. total foreign trade with all nations, detail for trade with particular nations and regions of the world, as well as for individual commodities. Using the report, the importance of one country's economy may be analyzed in terms of U.S. trade. The report can further reveal to what extent overseas growth is contributing to the U.S. economic performance.

ISM Index

The Institute for Supply Management (ISM) releases a monthly composite index based on surveys of 300 purchasing managers nationwide, representing 20 industries regarding manufacturing activity. Index values above 50 indicate an expanding economy, while values below 50 are indicative of contraction. The index is seasonally adjusted for the effects of variations within the year, differences due to holidays, and institutional changes. The index is a composite of nine similarly constructed indices, including: new orders, production, supplier delivery times, backlogs, inventories, prices, employment, export orders, and import orders. Information on activity in each of the 20 industries is provided separately. The ISM survey also provides price changes for 14 key inputs.

ISM Non-Manufacturing Index

The Institute for Supply Management (ISM) Non-Manufacturing Index is based on surveys of 370 purchasing and supply executives. The index is weighted to correspond with each industry's contribution to GDP. Index values over 50 percent indicate an expansion, while values below 50 percent indicate contraction. There are 10 separate indices reported, but business activity is considered the most important. The other nine indices are: new orders, supplier deliveries, employment, inventories, prices, backlog of orders, new export orders, imports, and inventory sentiment. The services industry is the largest component of the index. Other industries include construction, mining, and transportation among others.

Jobless Claims
See **Initial Jobless Claims**

Kansas City Fed Manufacturing Survey

The Federal Reserve Bank of Kansas City surveys roughly 300 manufacturing plants that are representative of the district's industrial and geographic makeup. Indices are calculated by subtracting the percentage of total respondents reporting decreases in a given indicator from the percentage of those reporting increases. The indices, which can range from 100 to -100, reveal the general direction of the indicators by showing how, or if, the number of plants with improving conditions offset those with worsening conditions. Index values greater than zero generally suggest expansion, while values less than zero indicate contraction.

Leading Economic Indicators

This Conference Board report is released on a monthly basis, reflecting economic data and indicators for the two months prior. Leading Indicators is comprised mostly of previously announced economic indicators such as new orders, jobless claims, money supply, average workweek, building permit, and stock prices. Therefore, the report is not seen as very predictive in nature.

Monthly Mass Layoffs

Mass layoff statistics are compiled by the Bureau of Labor Statistics from initial unemployment insurance claims. Each month, states report on establishments that have at least 50 initial unemployment insurance claims filed against them during a consecutive 5-week period regardless of duration. These establishments then are contacted by the state agency to determine whether these separations lasted 31 days or longer, and, if so, other information concerning the layoff is collected. Quarterly mass layoff reports include additional information. The report lists how many layoff events occurred and how many people who are eligible to receive unemployment compensation were affected. Layoff events are segmented by state and industry.

New Home Sales

The Bureau of the Census compiles data for this report from telephone or personal interviews of about 10,000 builders or owners of about 15,000 selected building projects. To provide nationwide coverage of building activity, a multistage stratified random sample procedure is used to select some 820 building permit-issuing offices and a sample of more than 70 land areas not covered by building permits.

New Residential Construction

New Residential Construction, released by the Bureau of the Census, provides statistics on the construction of new privately owned residential structures in the United States. Data include the number of new housing units authorized by building permits; the number of housing units authorized to be built, but not yet started; the number of housing units started; the number of housing units under construction; and the number of housing units completed. The data relate to new housing units intended for occupancy and maintained by the occupants. They exclude hotels, motels, and group residential structures, such as nursing homes and college dormitories. Also excluded are "HUD-code" manufactured (mobile) home units, and units that are created in an existing residential or nonresidential structure.

Personal Income

Personal Income from the Bureau of Economic Analysis mainly measures the income received by households from employment, self-employment, investments, and transfer payments. It also includes small amounts for expenses of nonprofit organizations and income of certain fiduciary activities. The largest component of personal income is wages and salaries from employment. Personal income is released after the employment report and thus can be estimated by the payroll and earnings data for the employment report. Disposable income refers to personal income after the payment of income, estate, certain other taxes, and payments to governments.

Philadelphia Fed Survey

Every month, the Federal Reserve Bank of Philadelphia surveys respondents to assess general business conditions as well as company business conditions. Answers are given based in the current month versus the previous month, and the outlook for 6 months from the current month. An indicator is presented for a decrease, no change, an increase, and a diffusion index.

Producer Price Index (PPI)

The Producer Price Index (PPI) from the Bureau of Labor Statistics is a family of indices that measures average changes in selling prices received by domestic producers for their output. The PPI tracks changes in prices for nearly every goods-producing industry in the domestic economy, including agriculture, electricity and natural gas, forestry, fisheries, manufacturing, and mining.

Productivity and Costs

Productivity and associated costs, compiled by the Bureau of Labor Statistics, reflects the relationship between real output and the labor and capital inputs involved in production. This shows changes over time in the amount of goods and services produced per unit of input.

Retail Sales

The Retail Sales report from the Bureau of Census includes merchandise sold (for cash or credit at retail or wholesale) by establishments primarily engaged in retail trade. Services that are incidental to the sale of merchandise, and excise taxes that are paid by the manufacturer or wholesaler and passed along to the retailer, are also included. Sales are net after deductions for refunds and allowances for merchandise returned by customers. Sales exclude sales taxes collected directly from the customer and paid directly to a local, state, or federal tax agency. The monthly retail trade estimates are developed from samples representing all sizes of firms and kinds of businesses in retail trade throughout the nation.

Richmond Fed Manufacturing Survey

The Federal Reserve Bank of Richmond surveys roughly 190 manufacturing plants that are representative of the district's industrial and geographic makeup. The indices are calculated by subtracting the percentage of total respondents reporting decreases in a given indicator from the percentage of those reporting increases. The indices, which can range from 100 to -100, reveal the general direction of the indicators by showing how the number of plants with improving conditions offset those with worsening conditions. Index values greater than zero generally suggest expansion, while values less than zero indicate contraction.

Risk of Recession

Economy.com produces a "Risk of Recession" leading indicator, composed of four state and metro area indicators, two broad regional indicators, and two national indicators. Because no single variable explains shifts in the business cycle, the variables are combined into a composite index. The components of the Economy.com regional leading index are as follows: housing permits (state or metro), manufacturing hours worked (state or metro), initial jobless claims (state only), trade-weighted index of the value of the dollar (state), help-wanted index (metro where available, census division elsewhere), consumer confidence (census division), S&P 500 stock index (national), and Treasury yield curve (national).

Semiconductor Book-to-Bill Ratio

Semiconductor Equipment and Materials International releases the results of a survey of U.S. manufacturers on a monthly basis. The 3-month moving average of shipments and new orders plus their ratio, named the book-to-bill ratio, are all included.

Semiconductor Billing

The Semiconductor Industry Association reports the global dollar volume of integrated circuit sales on a 3-month moving average on a monthly basis. All types of semiconductor chips are included in the totals: microprocessors, memory, and others. The sales are reported individually for four regions: North America, Asia-Pacific, Japan, and Europe. The data are compiled from a survey of the largest global chip manufacturers.

Senior Loan Officer Opinion Survey

The report is drawn from a survey of approximately 60 large domestic banks and 24 branches and agencies of foreign banks. The Federal Reserve generally conducts the survey quarterly, timing it so that results are available for the January, May, August, and November meetings of the Federal Open Market Committee. The Federal Reserve occasionally conducts one or two additional surveys during the year. Questions cover changes in the standards and terms of the banks' loans and the state of business and household demand for loans.

Treasury Budget

The U.S. Department of Treasury budget is a monthly account of the surplus or deficit of the U.S. government. Detailed information is provided on receipts and outlays of the federal government. The information is provided on a monthly and fiscal year-to-date basis.

Unemployment Rate

The unemployment rate is released by the Bureau of Labor Statistics, and represents the number unemployed as a percent of the labor force. Persons are classified as unemployed if they do not have a job, have actively looked for work in the prior 4 weeks, and are currently available for work. Actively looking for work may consist of any of the following activities: networking, contacting an employer directly, or having a job interview with a public or private employment agency; contacting a school or university employment center; sending out resumes or filling out applications; placing or answering advertisements; checking union or professional registers; or some other means of active job search. People are counted as employed if they did any work at all for pay or profit during the survey week. This includes all part-time and temporary work, as well as regular full-time year-round employment. Persons also are counted as employed if they have a job at which they did not work during the survey week because they were on vacation, experiencing child-care problems, taking care of some other family or personal obligation, on maternity or paternity leave; involved in an industrial dispute; or prevented from working by bad weather.

University of Michigan Consumer Sentiment Survey

The University of Michigan Consumer Research Center conducts a telephone survey of 500 consumers who are asked questions about personal finances, business conditions, and buying conditions. The survey employs a rotating panel design. Each month, 60 percent of the consumers are added to the sample for the first time, while the remaining are interviewed a second time. Households are asked five questions that include (1) a rating of household financial conditions, (2) a rating of expected household financial conditions a year from now, (3) a rating of expected business conditions a year from now, (4) expectations for the economy for the next 5 years, and (5) buying plans. The responses are seasonally adjusted. An index is constructed for each response and then a composite index is based on the responses.

Vehicle Sales

Auto companies report vehicle sales each month. Light vehicle sales are divided between cars and light trucks (sport utility vehicles, pickup trucks, and vans). Light vehicles sales include both sales of vehicles assembled in North America that are sold in the United States and sales of imported vehicles sold in the United States.

Wholesale Trade

Companies provide data to the Bureau of Census on dollar-values of merchant wholesale sales, end-of-month inventories, and methods of inventory valuation. Monthly wholesale trade, sales, and inventory reports are released 6 weeks after the close of the reference month. They contain preliminary current month figures and final figures for the previous month. Statistics include sales, inventories, and stock/sale ratios. Data is collected via a mail survey of about 7,100 selected wholesale firms. The sample is updated every quarter to add new businesses and eliminate those who are no longer active wholesalers.

ECONOMIC CALENDAR

Monday	Tuesday	Wednesday	Thursday	Friday
	1 Semiconductor Billings* 1 Challenger Report 2 Construction Spending (C30) 2 ISM Index 3	**2** Vehicle Sales - AutoData* 1 MBA Mortgage Applications Survey 1 ABC News/Money Magazine Consumer Comfort Index 2 Risk of Recession 2	**3** Chain Store Sales 3 Monster Employment Index 2 Jobless Claims 4 Productivity and Costs 3 Factory Orders (SIO or M3) 2 ISM Non-Mfg. Index 4 Oil and Gas Inventories 2 Weekly Natural Gas Storage Report 2	**4** Employment Situation 5 ECRI Future Inflation Gauge 3 ECRI Weekly Leading Index 1
7 Consumer Credit (G19) 1	**8** Creditforecast.com Quarterly Household Credit Report 1 Chain Store Sales Snapshot 2 Richmond Fed Manufacturing Survey 2	**9** MBA Mortgage Applications Survey 2 ABC News/Money Magazine Consumer Comfort Index 2 Job Openings and Labor Turnover Survey 2 Wholesale Trade (MWTR) 3 Oil and Gas Inventories 2	**10** Jobless Claims 4 Import and Export Prices 2 Weekly Natural Gas Storage Report 2 Treasury Budget* 3 ECRI Weekly Leading Index 1	**11**

Scale: 1 – Least Significant; 3 – Signficant; 5 – Highly Signficant

Monday	Tuesday	Wednesday	Thursday	Friday
14 Retail Sales (MARTS) **3** International Trade (FT900) **2** Kansas City Fed Manufacturing Survey **2**	**15** Chain Store Sales Snapshot **2** Consumer Price Index **3** Business Inventories (MTIS) **2** NY Empire State Manufacturing Survey **2** University of Michigan Consumer Sentiment Survey **3** NAHB Housing Market Index **2**	**16** MBA Mortgage Applications Survey **2** ABC News/Money Magazine Consumer Comfort Index **2** New Residential Construction (C20) **1** Industrial Production **2** Oil and Gas Inventories **2** Beige Book **4**	**17** Jobless Claims **4** The Conference Board Leading Indicators **1** Weekly Natural Gas Storage Report **2** Philadelphia Fed Survey **2** SEMI Book-to-Bill Ratio **2**	**18** Current Account **3** ECRI Weekly Leading Index **1**
21	**22** Chain Store Sales Snapshot **2**	**23** MBA Mortgage Applications Survey **2** ABC News/Money Magazine Consumer Comfort Index **2** Monthly Mass Layoffs **3** Oil and Gas Inventories **2**	**24** Jobless Claims **4** Durable Goods (Advance) **3** The Conference Board Help Wanted Index **2** New Home Sales (C25) **2** Weekly Natural Gas Storage Report **2**	**25** GDP **5** University of Michigan Consumer Sentiment Survey **3** Existing Home Sales **2** ECRI Weekly Leading Index **1**

Scale: 1 – Least Significant; 3 – Signficant; 5 – Highly Signficant

Monday	Tuesday	Wednesday	Thursday	Friday
28 Personal Income **3** UBS Index of Investor Optimism **1**	**29** Chain Store Sales Snapshot **2** The Conference Board Consumer Confidence **3** Agricultural Prices **2**	**30** MBA Mortgage Applications Survey **2** ABC News/Money Magazine Consumer Comfort Index **2** NAPM - NY Report **2** Chicago Fed National Activity Index **2** Chicago PMI **2** Oil and Gas Inventories **2**		

Scale: 1 – Least Significant; 3 – Signficant; 5 – Highly Signficant

RATINGS EXPLANATION

1 and 2—This data is marked as least significant because data release has little (if any) impact on the markets and is not a key measurement of the U.S. economy. Data marked with 1 or 2 has no role in Astor's economic model.

3—Data given the significant rating indicates that the data release has a limited impact on the markets, but may represent a key area of our economy. Data marked as 3 do not have a direct impact on Astor's economic model, but are closely monitored.

4 and 5—A highly significant rating indicates that the data is the most important to the market and represents a key component of the economy. Data that has a rating of 4 or 5 have a large influence on Astor's economic model.

RECOMMENDED READING

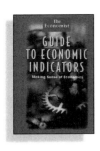

The Economist Guide to Economic Indicators: Making Sense of Economics

By The Economist. $34.95. Item #BC92-8448.

A blueprint for understanding economic information from all over the world. There is a critical need today for business executives, investors, and students to have a thorough knowledge of the economic indicators that are released every day and used throughout the world. The comprehensive primer addresses that need, clearly explaining each major indicator and how to interpret it.

The Wall Street Journal Guide to Understanding Money and Investing

By Kenneth M. Morris at al. $15.95. Item #BC92-11898.

If financial jargon seems like a foreign language, then this book is for you. *The Wall Street Journal Guide* covers everything from buying stocks and mutual funds to spotting trends. This quick and easy guide is all you need to get a clear understanding of what's going on in the world of finance.

▲ ▲ ▲ ▲ ▲ ▲

These books, and thousands of others, are available at:

www.FPBooks.com

The Irwin Guide to Using The Wall Street Journal, 6th Edition

By Michael B. Lehmann. $29.95.
Item #BC92-10602.

Now, updated to include the latest charts, examples, information on every facet of the investing world, sample articles and data taken directly from the pages of *The Journal* itself, this new guide provides an in-depth view of investment choices, the stock market, commodities, and the role of interest rates in the business cycles.

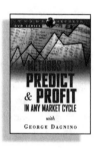

Methods to Predict & Profit in Any Market Cycle

By George Dagnino. $64.95. Item #BC92-982785.

Learn to profit in any type of market by mastering the key economic and investment forces that can affect your portfolio. By knowing what to look for, you'll be better poised to time your market moves and balance your portfolio for maximum returns. With full online support manual, this presentation by market veteran George Dagnino makes a great companion to his bestselling book *Profit in Bull and Bear Markets*.

▲ ▲ ▲ ▲ ▲ ▲

These books, and thousands of others, are available at:

www.FPBooks.com
Go there today and experience savings up to 70% off all books, videos, DVDs, and more!

Or call us at

1-800-272-2855 ext. BC92

FREE Catalog . . .

Take Advantage of Special Saving Offers:

- Bestsellers Up to 80% Off
- Big Savings on New Releases
- NEW Titles from Top Names
- Deep Discounts on EVERY ITEM
- Buy in Bulk for Clients— Save Even MORE!
- Great Gift Books
- Limited Quantities

Free 2 Week Trial Offer for U.S. Residents From Investor's Business Daily:

INVESTOR'S BUSINESS DAILY will provide you with the facts, figures, and objective news analysis you need to suceed.

Investor's Business Daily is formatted for a quick and concise read to help you make informed and profitable decisions.

> To take advantage of this 2 week trial offer,
> e-mail us at customerservice@fpbooks.com
> or visit our website at www.FPBooks.com where
> you find other free offers as well.
>
> You can also reach us by calling 1-800-272-2855
> or fax us at 410-964-0027

About the Author

ROBERT N. STEIN is the Managing Partner and Senior Economist of Astor Asset Management, LLC, a U.S. Securities and Exchange Commission registered investment advisory firm. A University of Michigan graduate in Economics, Mr. Stein was a project analyst for the Federal Reserve during the chairmanship of Paul Volcker. Moving to Wall Street, he became a Senior Trader for Bank of America and Barclay's Bank BZW, before returning to Chicago to establish an investment and brokerage firm.

In 2003, Mr. Stein was named one of "The Best Unknown Managers" by *BusinessWeek Magazine*. Frequently featured in the news media, Mr. Stein has been interviewed by CNN, CNBC, Bloomberg TV and is a regular guest on Fox News. He is interviewed frequently by *Investor's Business Daily*, *The New York Times*, and *The Wall Street Journal*. Mr. Stein is also the author of *Inside Greenspan's Briefcase: Investment Strategies for Profiting from Key Reports & Data* (McGraw-Hill, 2002).

Astor Asset Management, LLC, is a U.S. Securities & Exchange Commission-registered investment advisory firm that specializes in individually managed accounts. Astor believes that active management is the key to success in any investment portfolio. Through active management, investors can profit as markets move and trend in both directions. Astor's goal is to accomplish superior returns with less risk during various market conditions.

Its investment programs base their investment strategies on analysis of economic indicators, overall market conditions and money flows. For more information about Astor or to contact Robert N. Stein, Portfolio Manager and Managing Partner, please see the Astor Asset Management web site at www.astorllc.com.

This book, along with other books, are available at discounts that make it realistic to provide them as gifts to your customers, clients, and staff. For more information on these long-lasting, cost-effective premiums, please call John Boyer at 800-272-2855 or e-mail him at john@fpbooks.com